W9-BSF-569

Mine Eyes Have Seen the
GLORY

GORDON FERGUSON

Mine Eyes Have Seen the
GLORY

The Victory of the Lamb
in the Book of
Revelation

2 Sterling Road
Billerica, MA 01862-2595
1-800-727-8273
Fax: (781) 937-3889

All Scripture quotations, unless indicated, are taken from
the HOLY BIBLE, NEW INTERNATIONAL VERSION.
Copyright © 1973, 1978, 1984 by the International Bible Society.
Used by permission of
Zondervan Publishing House. All rights reserved.

The "NIV" and "New International Version" trademarks are
registered in the United States Patent Trademark Office by the
International Bible Society. Use of either
trademarks requires the permission of the
International Bible Society.

Mine Eyes Have Seen the Glory

©1996 by Discipleship Publications International
2 Sterling Road, Billerica, MA 01862-2595

All rights reserved. No part of this book may be
duplicated, copied, translated, reproduced, or stored
mechanically or electronically without specific, written
permission of Discipleship Publications International.

Printed in the United States of America

Cover design: Chris Costello
Cover photography: Telegraph Colour Lib/FPG International Corp.
Interior layout: Chris Costello and Laura Root

ISBN 1-884553-92-3

*To the Boston church
whose commitment to Christ
and unconditional love for me
have helped me to see
His glory more clearly.*

Contents

Foreword

Mysterious. Confusing. Intriguing. Symbolic. Deep. Difficult. Literal. Futuristic. All these words and many others have been used to describe the final book of the Bible, Revelation.

Misunderstood. Misinterpreted. Misapplied. These words speak of the "missed" message of Revelation in light of today's prevailing humanism, hedonism and hypocrisy.

Inspiring. Crucial. Radical. Victorious. Compelling. Challenging. Thrilling. Strengthening. These are a few of the right words—God's initial intent—about what is to happen in our hearts and in our souls after spending time with the apostle John on the island of Patmos as he reveals God through this revelation. In *Mine Eyes Have Seen the Glory*, Gordon Ferguson unlocks and unleashes God's powerful and timeless message—a message that will forever revolutionize our lives!

Gordon Ferguson is a man who loves God. He is a man who seeks God. Presently, he is an elder and evangelist in the Boston church but, I believe, his greatest gift for God lies in being a teacher in the kingdom of God. Gordon is a world-class teacher who has made an impact on countless lives around the globe. We have worked together, prayed together, cried together and laughed together for many years. He is a true friend. I know his life and his family, and I commend Gordon Ferguson to everyone.

This book needs to be read by each disciple. More than that, this book needs to be taken into the heart of each disciple. For truly, there is a God who is in control of the universe! There is a deliverer from any trial or persecution. There is security because our victory is sure. Therefore, let us, as disciples, never stop, never give up, never give in, never retreat and never surrender! Read this book as you study Revelation. You will come face to face with God as never before and will find yourself joyfully shouting with the heavenly multitudes, "Mine eyes have seen the glory!"

Randy McKean
Boston, Massachusetts

Introduction

We use the term "persecution" to describe the social rejection we receive because we choose to be followers of Jesus. Although this treatment hurts our feelings, it is quite mild when contrasted with the way early Christians were treated. They would probably be amazed that we make so much of what amounts to mild rejection in the form of cold shoulders, gossip behind our backs, and at worst, insults to our faces. Our fellow Christians who first read or heard read the book of Revelation were facing unbelievable challenges and needed an unbelievable amount of help and encouragement.

Our first century brothers' and sisters' confession of Jesus as Lord and their unwavering loyalty to him had brought them into sharp conflict with their government. They were being discriminated against economically, socially and were beginning to be persecuted physically. Times were tough and Satan was doing his best to cause them to second-guess their stance for righteousness.

Picture a night meeting of disciples during such a time. On one side of a cave several women are talking in hushed, but emotional, tones. Mary was sharing how her grown son was thrown in jail two days ago because he would not deny Jesus publicly. Then yesterday, her husband was dragged away and tortured severely. He joined his son in jail afterwards. Now the reports are coming back from the authorities that both men are to be executed at dawn tomorrow.

How would you react if you were Mary? If her husband and son would simply say "Caesar is Lord" they could both be released. Perhaps in the long run, such an action would seem to be better. Certainly it would seem reasonable for men with families and responsibilities to preserve their lives in order to fulfill these responsibilities. And God would forgive them, wouldn't he? But Mary's men would not entertain the possibility of backing down from their commitment to Jesus. They remembered his words in Matthew 10:32-34:

> *"Whoever acknowledges me before men, I will also acknowledge him before my Father in heaven. But whoever disowns me before men, I will disown him before my Father in heaven.*

Do not suppose that I have come to bring peace to the earth. I did not come to bring peace, but a sword."

Now that Mary was facing the imminent deaths of her husband and son, what did she most need to hear? What did she most need to see? This account is fictional, but thousands of disciples in the first century could tell us actual stories just like it. Hearts were torn apart when the consequences of being hated by the world were meted out by hearts filled with poison. The book of Revelation was inspired by God to help hurting disciples cope with the realities of spiritual warfare for his name. They needed comfort, to be sure, but more than anything they needed to be lifted out of their physical dilemma into the spiritual presence of God himself. They needed to see everything from his perspective of eternity and to realize that no matter what ensued on earth, heaven is real and heaven's inhabitants are participants in the battle along with them.

Whatever difficulty we may have in trying to interpret Revelation, it must be remembered that its first readers not only had great needs for encouragement but they also had the helpful familiarity with apocalyptic writings to help them gain that encouragement. For us the basic message may seem obscured by the symbolism, but it can be comprehended if we are willing to "dig in." For that purpose, this exposition is written.

To the reader of the book of Revelation come great blessings. Is it difficult to fully understand? Yes. But no one can read the book without being struck by the very theme and purpose of it: *Christ is Lord and Victorious Ruler and he and his church will live eternally in the "New Jerusalem,"* heaven. It is a book of cheer, consolation, comfort, encouragement and confident victory to the Christian; but, on the other hand, it is a book of despair, ruin and tragic destruction for those who are evil, unbelieving, or unfaithful to Christ. If our hearts are affected by Revelation in the way God intends, we will be more determined than ever to spread the message of life and death and heaven and hell to all parts of the globe, no matter what the temporal consequences! Jesus is the Lord of lords and the King of kings, the Alpha and the Omega, the bright Morning Star, the Root and Offspring of David, the One who was, who is and who is to come! Believe it, trust it, live it and shout it out to a lost earth, for the glory of God!

1
▼

Can This *Strange* Book Really Be Understood?
INTERPRETATION ISSUES

To express a belief that one can truly understand the book of Revelation—this book of symbols—is certain to attract some incredulous looks. However, God would not include a book in his word that could not be understood. To do so would be contrary to the very purpose of Scripture (Ephesians 3:2-5). Revelation, properly viewed, is an incredible book of impact. Because of its style and content, it is often called the "Grand Finale" of the Bible. Revelation's literary structure, beautiful imagery, majestic visions, mysterious symbols, and dramatic presentation of eternal truths, make this book distinctive from all other books of the Bible.

Revelation is the English translation of the Greek word *apokalupsis*, meaning "to reveal or uncover that which has been hidden." Revelation is classified as "apocalyptic" literature by scholars. Such literature was popular for about 200 years before Christ and for about 100 years after him. It has the following characteristics:

1. It addresses those undergoing some form of persecution.
2. It addresses the reader in the nuances and style of the language and time period in which it is written.
3. It is dramatic and highly symbolic (expressed in visions and symbols).
4. It is sometimes predictive, although the basic message is focused on the circumstances of the time when it was written.
5. It is practical, written to meet particular spiritual needs of people.

The book of Revelation is similar to parts of Old Testament (OT) prophetic books such as Ezekiel and Daniel. In fact, much of Revelation cannot be understood without a basic knowledge of the Old Testament and its phraseology. But this relationship should not cause us to think that Revelation is the *fulfillment* of OT prophecy. Rather, it uses a similar style to describe the ultimate downfall of heathen nations and the exaltation of God's kingdom. Similar symbols may be used in the OT books, but they are describing very different events—events separated by hundreds of years.

Apocalyptic language is used to create a dramatic effect. It appeals to the imagination more than the intellect. In times of persecution, those who are suffering need the inspiration that comes from hearing about God's conclusive triumph over evil far more than they need academic pronouncements of doctrine. With this in mind, understanding symbolic language is much like understanding parables—get the main points and avoid overanalyzing the details. If more commentary writers and theologians followed this approach, sensationalistic interpretations would be greatly reduced, thus limiting the abounding confusion about Revelation.

No book in the Bible has resulted in more contradictory interpretations than the book of Revelation. It is likely that more false ideologies have arisen from a misunderstanding of this book than from any other portion of the Scriptures. In studying such a book, we would be better off to first consider what it *does not teach* rather than what it *does teach!* One study rule must be remembered when studying any book in the Bible, namely that an easily understood passage must not be explained by a difficult or symbolic passage. We must let the "easy" passage interpret the "difficult" one. Therefore, Revelation should be studied in close harmony with the rest of the Scriptures.

General Background

The original recipients of Revelation were the disciples in the seven churches of Asia: Ephesus, Smyrna, Pergamum, Thyatira, Sardis, Philadelphia and Laodicea (Revelation 1:11). However, what was written to one or all of these churches is also intended for all the Lord's churches. "He who has an ear, let him hear what the Spirit says to the churches" (2:7). The same point is made in the conclusion of the short letter to each of the seven churches. Revelation 1:3 pronounces a blessing upon anyone who hears and keeps the words of this book— "Blessed is the one who reads the words of this prophecy, and blessed are those who hear it and take to heart what is written in it, because the time is near."

The title "Revelation," comes from verse 1 of the first chapter. This verse says that the revelation came from Christ and was given to him by God, for the purpose of making it known to his servants. This message was then sent by an angel to John, who was commanded to write it in a scroll (1:11). Therefore, from its inception, Revelation is presented as a document intended to be understood by its readers. It is designed to be a mystery only in the Biblical sense—something once concealed but now revealed (see Ephesians 3:2-5).

The writer, John the apostle, states that Jesus commanded him to write (1:10-11, 19). John describes himself as "your brother and companion in the suffering and kingdom and patient endurance that are ours in Jesus" (1:9). Furthermore he informs us that when he received the revelation he was exiled on the island of Patmos (1:9). Tradition has it that he was the only apostle who died a natural death. All the others were supposedly killed as martyrs. An interesting side note concerns John's age. If he received the revelation in his late eighties or early nineties, as seems to be the case, he must have been very young when he was called as an apostle—quite possibly a teenager! He is, of course, the same John who also wrote the Gospel and the three short letters, all of which bear his name.

The various dates assigned by conservative scholars to the writing of Revelation range from 68 to 96 AD. Scholars offer different arguments to support their choices, but the majority settle on 95-96 AD. John explains in Revelation 1:9 that he was "on the island of Patmos, because of the word of God and the testimony of Jesus." Irenaeus, wrote in about 175 AD that this banishment of John to Patmos was during Emperor Domitian's reign (81-96 AD). We can be reasonably sure that this was the time period during which the book was written or at least circulated. When we come to Revelation 17:10-11, we will discuss the possibility that the book was written slightly earlier and then circulated during the reign of Domitian. If this possibility is accepted, Revelation would be a prophecy in the sense normally thought of by anticipating this period of persecution.

The main objective of John's writing was to comfort persecuted Christians. God wanted them to know that their tears did not go unnoticed (7:17, 21:4). On the contrary, their prayers moved God to act (8:3-4). Even in the face of death, he wanted them to know that persecution—this ultimate way of suffering—was special to him and would not go unrewarded.

> *Then I heard a voice from heaven say, "Write: Blessed are the dead who die in the Lord from now on."*
> *"Yes," says the Spirit, "they will rest from their labor, for their deeds will follow them." (Revelation 14:13)*

Their final victory is assured (15:2) and their blood will be avenged (6:9-17). Christ is the key to providing the encouragement needed to face persecution, for he rules forever (5:11-13) and is coming again to receive his own (chapters 21, 22).

? By now, you have figured out that studying Revelation is going to demand serious concentration and mental energy. How do you feel about that? Are you the type who wants everything to be very simple and quickly understandable, or do you enjoy digging for buried treasure? What type of attitudes toward study should you have? Why?

Symbolism

Revelation is filled with symbols including animals, men, heavenly beings, colors, aspects of nature and numbers. For example the two beasts introduced in chapter 13 can be seen as representing two different aspects of the Roman Empire. To the informed reader the specific colors of the four horses in chapter 6 convey a deeper level of meaning than the literal text. Red is the symbolic color of persecution and the bloodshed that accompanies it, and white is the color of purity and victory. The use of numbers is especially important and can often be misunderstood. While numerology in Jewish literature of the period is not an exact science, we can generally say that numbers were used in the following ways:

1) *One* signifies unity. The seven "ones" in Ephesians 4:4-6 fall into Paul's platform of developing and maintaining unity. In Revelation 17:13, we read: "They have one purpose and will give their power and authority to the beast."

2) *Two* conveys the idea of strength. For example, Jesus sent out disciples two by two (Mark 6:7, Luke 10:1). Revelation 11:3 states: "And I will give power to my two witnesses, and they will prophesy for 1,260 days, clothed in sackcloth."

3) *Three* is the divine number. Although not used directly in this sense in Revelation, it is involved in a very important combination to get the number "7."

4) *Four* represents the world or cosmos. In Revelation, we find the four living creatures (4:6), four angels, four corners of the earth, and four winds of heaven (7:1).

5) *Seven* denoting perfection is obtained by adding the "divine" number three and the "cosmic" number four. The number seven is found in Revelation over *fifty* times! In 4:5, the "seven spirits of God" refers to the Holy Spirit in his perfection. "The seven churches of Asia" were literal churches, but the use of seven also symbolized the entire church of the first century with its various strengths and weaknesses.

— 6) *Six,* falling just short of the perfect *seven,* was viewed as an evil and sinister number. It was viewed much as the number thirteen is in our day. Modern American hotels normally do not designate a thirteenth floor because of the superstition involved. If a multistoried building were built in the first century, it would most surely not have had a sixth floor!

7) *Ten* represents completeness. For example, if a person had all ten fingers and all ten toes, he was considered complete. Revelation 17:12 mentions ten kings and ten horns, showing a completeness in their reign.

8) *One thousand,* a multiple of ten ($10 \times 10 \times 10$) is the number of ultimate completeness. It is a common symbolic number in the Bible. Exodus 20:6, reads "but showing love to a thousand generations of those who love me and keep my commandments." God is not limiting his love to a literal 1,000 generations, becoming unloving to the 1,001st! When he says "for every animal of the forest is mine, and the cattle on a thousand hills" (Psalm 50:10), he is not saying that the cattle on the 1,001st hill and beyond belong to someone else. This

has great impact on the interpretation of Jesus' thousand year reign, as we will see when we come to Revelation 20.

9) *Twelve*, the product of four and three, represents God's spiritual groups or organizations. In the Old Testament, the twelve tribes of Israel were the foundation of the Jewish people. In the Gospels, Jesus chose twelve apostles. Revelation mentions both the tribes and the apostles (21:12, 14). In Revelation 7, the tribes are not intended to be the literal Jewish ones, but in context, are signifying the redeemed followers of the Christ.

10) *144,000* is a multiple of one thousand (completeness) and twelve (God's people) (12 × 12 × 1,000 = 144,000). In Revelation 7 and 14, the 144,000 represents the full number of persecuted disciples. Again, it is not intended to be interpreted literally. Several factors in the specific texts will demonstrate the validity of this statement, as we will later see.

11) *Three and a half*, which is half of the perfect seven, designates a period of instability during the persecution. Variations of this number found in Revelation include 42 months and 1,260 days (both equaling three-and-a-half years), and from the Book of Daniel, "a time, times, and half of a time" (Daniel 7:25, 12:7).

Before you proceed with the various theories of interpreting Revelation, take the time to write out some of your present concepts. Specifically, what do you believe about the time of Jesus' second coming? Do you think we are in the "end times" now? Why or why not? How would you describe the book of Revelation to a friend who asked you about it?

Theories of Interpretation

As we begin explaining the main approaches to interpreting Revelation, you may feel a bit confused at times. However, as you continue to examine the bits and pieces more, you will grasp the essential ideas. You do not need to become an expert of interpretation to understand John's writings, but you should develop a basic understanding of how different writers and teachers have explained those writings. Virtually all of us have been influenced in our thinking about Revelation by these explanations, and much of what we have heard is incorrect. In order to replace erroneous views with correct ones, it is very helpful to first learn more about the systems of interpretation which are fraught with problems. Then, as a more accurate exposition is given, it will make itself evident with a solid "ring of truth."

Continuous Historical View

The continuous historical view considers the book to be primarily a blueprint of the history of Western Civilization. It places the symbols in chronological order and focuses on the Roman Catholic Church. It says God was giving John a picture of things that would happen over the following fifteen or twenty centuries. Most Protestant commentators around the time of the Reformation and thereafter, such as Albert Barnes and Adam Clarke, took this view.

Its weaknesses are many—chief of which is that it limits the events mainly to Western Civilization, thus removing the book from its first century setting and the intense problems faced by the disciples in these churches. Another difficulty comes in interpreting the last part of Revelation. Commentators often like to assign themselves and their era to the events that occur at the end of Revelation, (the time preceding the second coming of Christ). Subsequent interpreters, therefore, always need to change their interpretation of the various events to fit their particular day. A final weakness of this theory lies in its inconsistent interpretation of the symbols themselves. One type of symbol is interpreted one way in one case and in a very different way in another case. Trying to maintain a rigid sequential view allows nothing else.

An example of this interpretation by Albert Barnes, a mid-1800s commentator, is included below.[1] For purposes of illustration, I will include his interpretation of three of the more prominent *series* of symbols—the seals, the trumpets and the bowls of wrath.

1. First seal, a white horse (6:1-2)—from the death of Domitian to the accession of Commodus (96-180 AD).
2. Second seal, a red horse (6:3-4)—civil strife from the death of Commodus forward (193 AD).
3. Third seal, a black horse (6:5-6)—calamity from the time of Caracalla forward (211 AD).
4. Fourth seal, a pale horse (6:7-8)—bloodshed and famine during the time of Decius, Gallus, Emilianus, Valerian, and Gallianus (243-268 AD).

5. Fifth seal, the martyrs (6:9-11)—persecution of Christians, especially during the reign of Diocletian (284-304 AD).
6. Sixth seal, earthquake judgment (6:12-17)—threatened invasions of the Goths and Huns (and forward) (365 AD).
7. First trumpet (8:7)—Roman empire invaded by Alaric, king of the Goths (395-410 AD).
8. Second trumpet (8:8-9)—Roman empire invaded by Genseric, king of the Vandals (428-468 AD).
9. Third trumpet (8:10-11)—Roman empire invaded by Attila, king of the Huns (433-453 AD).
10. Fourth trumpet (8:12-13)—final conquest of Roman empire by Odoacer, king of the Heruli (476-490 AD).
11. Fifth trumpet (9:1-12)—the Mohammedans in power in the Eastern Empire.
12. Sixth trumpet (9:13-19)—the Turks in power in the Eastern Empire.
13. First bowl (16:1-2)—the first blow struck on the Papacy in the French Revolution.
14. Second bowl (16:3)—scenes of blood and carnage in that Revolution.
15. Third bowl (16:4-7)—French invasions of Northern Italy.
16. Fourth bowl (16:8-9)—later wars against the countries which had sustained the papal power.
17. Fifth bowl (16:10-11)—direct assault on the papal power; capture of the Pope himself.
18. Sixth bowl (16:12-16)—decline of the Turkish power; the rallying of the strength of Paganism, Mohammedanism and Romanism, represented by the three frogs that come out of the mouth of the dragon, beast and false prophet.
19. Seventh bowl (16:17-21)—complete and final overthrow of the Papal power.

From looking at the symbols and the interpretation, it is quite difficult to ascertain just how these symbols correlate with what Barnes says. This kind of interpretation is shallow at best and harmful at worst. If you were a first century disciple being persecuted for your faith, a history lesson about people and events that had absolutely no connection with your plight would be of little comfort. I am aware of no modern-day commentator who uses this theory of interpretation, which is not surprising.

Futurist View

The futurist view, unlike the previous theory, has multitudes of modern adherents. However, the variations among them are numerous. Conservative scholarship is definitely weighted toward this futurist view, despite the many variations. But, remember, the popularity of a view does not make it correct. The futurist view takes the position that most of the events described in the book are the "end times" just prior to Christ's return. Thus, this theory claims that most of the prophecy in the book is yet unfulfilled. On a popular level, Hal Lindsey has done more than anyone else to promote this view among the masses, through books like *The Late Great Planet Earth*,[2] one of the best-selling books of the 1970s.

Many of the symbols, especially numbers, are taken literally. Most futurists are also "premillennialists," meaning that they believe Jesus will return to earth *before* setting up a millennial reign from Jerusalem. Common aspects of many premillennialists are:

1. Christ will return to earth and rule for a literal 1,000 years.
2. Seven years before Christ's return, the righteous will experience a "rapture" (a "catching up," from the Latin word *raptio* in 1 Thessalonians 4:17) from the earth, while those left on earth will experience the "Great Tribulation" in the latter half of the seven-year period.
3. An Antichrist will arise to bring on the Great Tribulation.
4. At the end of the seven-year period, Jesus will return to set up his kingdom.
5. The church is not the actual kingdom Jesus came to establish. At best, it is a parenthetical aspect of the kingdom which is certainly not the fulfillment of OT prophecies.

The futurist view has found a remarkable acceptance in our day. A hundred years ago, it was rejected by most conservative evangelical scholars, but now most embrace it. The

Dallas Theological Seminary, Hal Lindsey's alma mater, and other institutions have successfully swayed the Biblical interpretations of many in this direction. However, the theories contained in the futurist view are based on very shaky Biblical ground. The reasons for the acceptance of the doctrine are not scriptural ones, as we shall show.

Due to the popularity of the view, some overall observations will be helpful at this point; we will look at other aspects of the doctrine of premillennialism when we come to the exposition of Revelation.

Two basic assumptions of the average futurist are worth noting at this point, and both are contradicted by Scripture. The first has to do with the nature of the kingdom that Jesus came to establish. Was it intended to be a spiritual kingdom or a physical one? The futurists assume the latter while the Bible teaches the former. The second assumption has to do with the second coming of Christ and the end of the world.

What Type of Kingdom?

The Jews expected their long-awaited Messiah to be a political king who would establish a physical kingdom. When they saw the miraculous power of Jesus, they were convinced he would fulfill their expectations. However, Jesus did not have the same agenda as those of his day (and the futurists of our day). "Jesus, knowing that they intended to come and make him king by force, withdrew again to a mountain by himself" (John 6:15). To the extreme disappointment of the Jews, he made it clear that his kingdom was not to be a physical one.

> Once, having been asked by the Pharisees when the kingdom of God would come, Jesus replied, "The kingdom of God does not come with your careful observation, nor will people say, 'Here it is,' or 'There it is,' because the kingdom of God is within you." (Luke 17:20-21)

In other words, they were not going to see his armies marching into Jerusalem to free them from Roman occupation.

Surely Jesus could not make it any clearer than he did with these words: "My kingdom is not of this world. If it were, my servants would fight to prevent my arrest by the Jews. But now my kingdom is from another place" (John 18:36). He did not deny being a king and having a kingdom; he simply denied their views of the nature of both. His focus on a spiritual kingdom was one of the primary reasons he was rejected. If he had come to do what the futurists believe, he would have been much more accepted among the Jews of his day.

The idea that OT prophecy is focused on a physical kingdom is Biblically unsound. The church is the kingdom of God on earth, not some parenthetical organization with an inferior role until the *real* kingdom is established when Jesus returns. The redemptive work of our Lord is at the very heart of Biblical prophecy. Listen to Christ's own words on this subject:

> *"...This is what I told you while I was still with you: Everything must be fulfilled that is written about me in the Law of Moses, the Prophets and the Psalms."*
>
> *Then he opened their minds so they could understand the Scriptures. He told them, "This is what is written: The Christ will suffer and rise from the dead on the third day, and repentance and forgiveness of sins will be preached in his name to all nations, beginning at Jerusalem." (Luke 24:44-47)*

All of what was prophesied about him and his mission in the Old Testament had to do with man's salvation beginning in the first century—not with the re-establishment of an earthly Davidic kingdom for a thousand-year reign at some future point.

Paul, the inspired apostle, focused precisely on the same teaching as seen in Colossians 1:12-14:

> *...giving thanks to the Father, who has qualified you to share in the inheritance of the saints in the kingdom of light. For he has rescued us from the dominion of darkness and brought us into the kingdom of the Son he loves, in whom we have redemption, the forgiveness of sins.*

The opportunity to have redemption through Jesus and to be in his kingdom was within reach during Paul's ministry in the first century. He was not speaking of events thousands of years in the future.

The Nature of the Second Coming

The second assumption of the premillennialists relates to the second coming of Christ and the end of the world. When he comes, there will be only one resurrection of the dead, not two or more as claimed by most futurists. A popular bumper sticker reads: "In case of Rapture, this car will be unmanned." When Jesus comes to raise us all up, *every* car will be unmanned! The good and the bad are raised simultaneously, and then will all be judged (John 5:28-29). Contrary to popular theory, there simply cannot be two separate resurrections. The righteous are raised on the *last day* (John 6:40) and the unrighteous are judged on the *last day* (John 12:48). Is not the last day really the last day? Furthermore, at the last trumpet, the dead are raised and the living are forever changed (1 Corinthians 15:51-52). If the wicked are raised a thousand years later, they will not be awakened by the last trumpet, for it will have already sounded!

In spite of its popularity, the futurist view is at serious odds with Scripture. It not only fails to deal honestly with Revelation in its original setting—it often contradicts other Biblical passages. Interesting and intriguing it may be, but Biblically accurate it is not.

Historical Background View

The historical background approach sees Revelation as a message addressed primarily to the disciples in the early church who were undergoing intense persecution by the Roman Empire. Two related approaches, the philosophy of history view and the preterist view, are often used in connection with the historical background view, but because of their similarities it is not necessary to detail them separately.

The Philosophy of History approach views the visions and symbols as a series of visionary descriptions of God's triumph over evil through the centuries. Thus, the book is concerned with inspiring courage in the church in its constant struggle with evil, regardless of the specific historical setting. However, most writers of this persuasion would still consider the historical events of the first century to be relevant in understanding the book. The basic interpretation of the symbolism involved is generally free of excesses, but is not as specific as the historical setting of persecution in the early church would warrant.

The Preterist (meaning "past") position holds that the bulk of Revelation has already been fulfilled in the days of the Roman Empire. Some preterist commentators would allow enough latitude for the latter part of the book to be taken as a description of the Judgment Day and eternity beyond it. Therefore, whereas the philosophy of history view sees Revelation as a general description of the ongoing battle between good and evil with the early church finding some application, the preterist view sees it as a specific description of the early church locked in battle with the Roman persecution.

As you can see, the differences between the philosophy of history and the preterist positions are not highly significant. Parts of both are obviously true. Therefore, it seems best to consider them as variations of the historical background view. The book does arise out of a specific historical setting of persecution, but the lessons the early disciples needed are also needed by disciples throughout the centuries as they face similar circumstances, especially persecution. Actually, every other NT book was written with a primary application to the first-century church. Since Scripture is "living and active," it is highly applicable to every generation, especially when those same needs and problems arise.

When all things are considered, the historical background view squares much more with the milieu out of which Revelation originated. It may not be as "mysterious" as you may have expected going into the study, but truth is the cure for speculation gone wild. Examine the explanations provided with Bible in hand, carefully checking out context and cross-references. Truth will make itself known, and you will be richly rewarded for seeking it in this unusual finale of the Bible.

The Historical Setting

A working knowledge of the historical setting of the early church is absolutely imperative to understanding the book of Revelation. The Roman system paved the way for the rapid spread of the Gospel, and it also paved the way for the rapid spread of persecution against that same Gospel. But all of the prophecies in the Old Testament were unquestionably pointing forward to this time in history when God chose to begin his new kingdom on earth in approximately 33 AD.

When Jesus, the Messiah, came, all of secular and sacred history merged. At the precise time appointed by God—"in the fullness of the time" (Galatians 4:4, King James Version)— Jesus was born of a woman. When all of the world events were lined up according to the eternal plan of God, then the Christ could be born, the One to whom the entire Old Testament pointed. It is highly important to see God's hand in all of this, and to see the integral connection between the *fullness* of time and the unavoidable *badness* of time when persecution produced the shed blood of Christians.

The ancient Greek culture contributed much to the preparation of the world for the coming of Christ and his church. One very important factor was the spread of the Greek language all over the empire. The *koine* (common) Greek language was similar to the use of English in our world today: just about everyone understood it, even the average man on the street. God chose this language as the medium to communicate the Gospel of his Son to the world. Little did Alexander the Great realize how his passion to spread the Greek culture throughout his empire would serve to speed the spread of Christianity throughout the same world in the later Roman times.

A related event during the Greek period was the translation of the Hebrew Old Testament into the Septuagint (the Greek version of the Old Testament) in Alexandria, Egypt. Jewish scholars felt the need for this translation because the Greek language had become the universal language, and many Hebrews were losing the use of their own language. The Septuagint (often abbreviated with the letters LXX because seventy scholars were commissioned to make the translation) became the Bible of most Jews and was often the version quoted by the NT writers.

Rome also contributed to the "fullness of time" mentioned above. The peace brought about by the Roman empire (*Pax Romana*) allowed the early missionaries to travel freely to promote their message. The seas were largely safe from the threat of piracy, and the roads were free from bandits. The Roman road system linked the empire in an unprecedented way. Significant remnants of some of the roads, such as the Appian Way and the Ignatian Way, survive even today. The ease of travel over long distances was not rivaled in our world until modern times. The common monetary system was another factor which made the mission of the church easier. The immoral climate of Rome made the light of the gospel shine all the brighter. Apart from Judaism and Christianity, religion and morality were in decline. Roman society was decadent, to put it mildly. Up to half the population was enslaved, and most others were poor.[3]

Taking all the above factors into account, when the gospel of Jesus began to be proclaimed, it found immediate receptivity and could be spread all over the known world in a matter of a few decades. But as the gospel penetrated the Roman world, an inevitable conflict resulted. The Roman government would not tolerate the spread of Christianity. The persecution that followed is the background for the book of Revelation.

The Roman Persecution

The conflict between Rome and the church was actually a conflict between two concepts of deity—the Romans believed in the *Dea Roma* (the goddess Rome) and the Christians believed in God. Her citizens were awed by Rome's power and the ensuing blessings of being a part of such a powerful nation. Years before the birth of Christ, the empire itself had begun to be deified as a spiritual entity. However, what began as a spirit of nationalism led to the worship of the head of state, the emperor.

The deification of a system or the leader of a system may seem strange to our modern ears, but we must keep in mind that idolatry was the norm. Many gods or goddesses were worshipped, and adding one more was not a challenge to the idolatrous philosophy, especially since this addition could readily be *seen*!

Julius Caesar was deified after his death by the loyalists in the Roman senate in 42 BC. Other emperors received similar exaltation after their deaths. Caligula, who was emperor from 37-41 AD, insisted on being worshipped as a god, but it was Domitian (81-96 AD), who demanded he be addressed as "Lord and God," and who first prompted widespread persecution against Christians. Eventually, to be a loyal citizen of Rome required the burning of incense and declaration "Caesar is

Lord." At this point Christians were totally flushed out into the light of public scrutiny for their refusal to ever acknowledge any lord other than Jesus. The die was cast, because to a follower of Jesus there would ever be only one Lord! Persecution and death were inevitable for disciples.[4]

The cause of persecution was obvious—light and darkness were locked in mortal combat. As Jesus put it,

> *"If the world hates you, keep in mind that it hated me first. If you belonged to the world, it would love you as its own. As it is, you do not belong to the world, but I have chosen you out of the world. That is why the world hates you." (John 15:18-19)*

However, the actual charges brought against the early Christians were quite different from the reason given by Jesus. Understanding the sources of the charges will help us to understand the development of persecution.

1. Christians refused to worship the emperor. This charge, unlike many others, was quite literally true and was the straw that broke the camel's back.
2. Christianity had a negative financial impact on those connected with idol worship (see Acts 19:23-36).
3. The majority of disciples were from the lower classes of society and were thus "not respectable." (See 1 Corinthians 1:26-29.)
4. Disciples of Jesus were first seen as a part of Judaism, and Jews were hated by the Romans because of their disdain of all who were *not* Jewish.
5. Christianity was a *religio illicita* (an illegal religion). When a province became a part of the Roman empire, existing religions were acceptable, but not new ones (especially those which actively sought converts!). At first, Christianity was seen as merely a sect of Judaism (Acts 28:22), but eventually it came to be seen as a new—hence illegal—movement.
6. Christianity was an exclusive religion. Other religions were condemned by Christians as false. Actually, the exclusivity caused them to be labeled as "atheists" because they did not worship the *gods*.

7. Christians were accused of evil practices ranging from cannibalism (because of the Lord's Supper—eating the body and drinking the blood of someone) to immorality (because of the affection demonstrated through "holy kisses" and terms of endearment).
8. Christians were viewed as fanatics because of their enthusiasm, which was clearly out of vogue among the passive philosophers of the day.

Against this backdrop, the book of Revelation was written.

2
▼

Enter King Jesus!
REVELATION 1

Revelation 1 introduces the book by introducing its *Star*—the bright Morning Star, Jesus Christ (Revelation 22:16). In the book, he is described in many marvelous ways which make our hearts soar with faith in him and calms us with comfort. The key to accepting persecution gracefully is to see Jesus as he really is—the all-powerful Risen Lord. This first chapter moves us purposefully in that direction. He revealed the nature of the spiritual struggle with the persecuting Roman empire, but more importantly, he revealed his true nature which guarantees victory over the onslaught of Satan himself!

> *[1:1]The revelation of Jesus Christ, which God gave him to show his servants what must soon take place. He made it known by sending his angel to his servant John, [2]who testifies to everything he saw—that is, the word of God and the testimony of Jesus Christ. [3]Blessed is the one who reads the words of this prophecy, and blessed are those who hear it and take to heart what is written in it, because the time is near.*

From verse one, it seems obvious that Jesus subscribed to the old adage, "To be forewarned is to be forearmed." (See John 16:1-4 for a similar advance warning.) He never paints a rosy picture of what it means to be his disciple. Reality must be faced if reality is to be overcome.

The basic message of the book involves events which must soon take place (1:1). Relegating the message to a far-distant point called the "end times" is therefore out of the question. Note similar statements in other verses: "the time is near" (1:3); "Do not seal up the words of the prophecy of this book, because the time is near" (22:10); and "He who testifies to these things says, 'Yes, I am coming soon'" (22:20). The bulk of the book describes events being faced by its first recipients.

Verse three gives us the first of seven beatitudes (not a surprising number!). As would be expected, they are full of comfort and inspiration for persecuted disciples. The basic thrust of each is as follows:

1. Blessed is he that reads this prophecy (1:3).
2. Blessed are the dead who die in the Lord (14:13).
3. Blessed is he who watches and is prepared for the Lord's coming (16:15).
4. Blessed are those invited to the Lamb's marriage supper (19:9).
5. Blessed is he who has part in the first resurrection (20:6).
6. Blessed is he who keeps the words of this book (22:7).
7. Blessed are they that wash their robes (or "do his commandments" in the KJV–22:14).

> ⁴*John,*
> *To the seven churches in the province of Asia:*
> *Grace and peace to you from him who is, and who was, and who is to come, and from the seven spirits before his throne,* ⁵*and from Jesus Christ, who is the faithful witness, the first-born from the dead, and the ruler of the kings of the earth.*
> *To him who loves us and has freed us from our sins by his blood,* ⁶*and has made us to be a kingdom and priests to serve his God and Father—to him be glory and power for ever and ever! Amen.*
> ⁷*Look, he is coming with the clouds,*
> *and every eye will see him,*
> *even those who pierced him;*
> *and all the peoples of the earth*
> *will mourn because of him.*
> *So shall it be! Amen.*
> ⁸*"I am the Alpha and the Omega," says the Lord God, "who is, and who was, and who is to come, the Almighty."*

The seven churches mentioned here each receive a letter from Jesus, which are found in the following two chapters of Revelation. The seven cities were located in the west-central part of the province of Asia Minor, its most influential region, being connected by a major road. The number "seven" here, although referring to seven literal cities, is still used in a symbolic manner, in that the entire church of Asia Minor is represented here, if not the whole church of the first century. In the next chapter, we will take an in-depth look at the condition of the first century kingdom (and be amazed at how little the challenges have changed from that day to ours).

The characteristic greeting, "grace and peace," (1:4) is given from Deity—the Father, the Spirit and the Son. The Father is called the one "who is, and who was, and who is to come," a reference to his eternal nature (1:4). He was introduced in Exodus 3:14 as "I AM," the eternally existing One. The Holy Spirit is designated as the "seven spirits" before God's throne, a way of designating the perfection of the Spirit. (See also 3:1, 4:5 and 5:6.) The Son is called a witness, the firstborn and a ruler. By this point in time, the word "witness" was starting to carry the meaning of "martyr," as may be seen in the case of Antipas in 2:13. Similarly, Jesus not only bore witness to God and his word (John 3:32, 8:14 and 18:37), but he was our faithful martyr on the cross.

The word "firstborn" has caused some to mistakenly believe that Jesus was a created being rather than a part of the eternal Deity. A similar passage is found in Colossians 1:15-18. Two things should be noted in this connection. First, in both passages Jesus is called the "firstborn from among the dead." In other words, he was given birth from the tomb in the resurrection. 1 Corinthians 15:20 calls him "the firstfruits of those who have fallen asleep." Therefore, the time reference relates to Jesus' rising from the dead. Second, the term "firstborn" (from the Greek *prototokos*) has to do with position. In Psalm 89:27, we read this statement about David: "I will also appoint him my firstborn, the most exalted of the kings of the earth." In Hebrew families the son born first always received a double portion of the family inheritance. Thus, "firstborn" came to refer to the position involved instead of the time per se. In Colossians 1:18, Jesus is also called "the beginning," but this word (from *arche*) likewise indicates position, meaning literally "power, principality or rule."

Jesus, as the ruler of the kings of the earth, has authority over every power precisely because he is *not* created—he is the eternal Word who became flesh (John 1:1-3, 14), and at that point, the Son. Therefore, the emperor who sat on Rome's throne was a presence, but not *the* Presence; a king, but not *the* King of kings. And this King has died to free us from our sins by his own blood, making us a part of his kingdom on earth, the church, and priests to our God. As priests, all Christians are to offer special sacrifices. Our first sacrifice is that of our bodies (Romans 12:1). Another is the "sacrifice of praise—the fruit of our lips that confess his name" (Hebrews 13:15). Also mentioned in the next verse is the sacrifice of doing good and sharing with those in need. Philippians 4:15-18 describes financial giving as a sacrifice. Finally, Paul depicts the saving of souls as an offering acceptable to God (Romans 15:15-16). Based on these descriptions of our priesthood, what kind of a priest have you been lately?

In 1:7, the "coming with the clouds" most naturally makes us think of the second coming, but this idea may not be the only one being conveyed. In fact, in light of 1:7 and 1:3, it probably is not even the *main* idea in view. The Bible often pictures God coming in temporal judgments in this way. For example, Isaiah 19:1 describes God's impending judgment of Egypt in these words:

An oracle concerning Egypt:

See, the LORD rides on a swift cloud
and is coming to Egypt.
The idols of Egypt tremble before him,
and the hearts of the Egyptians melt within them.

When Jesus described his judgment coming against Jerusalem in Mark 13:24-26 (which occurred in 70 AD), he said:

"But in those days, following that distress,

'the sun will be darkened,
and the moon will not give its light;
the stars will fall from the sky,
and the heavenly bodies will be shaken.'

At that time men will see the Son of Man coming in
clouds with great power and glory."

Some assume that Jesus is describing his second coming in this chapter and its parallels (Matthew 24 and Luke 21), but a closer examination of the specific questions Jesus was answering (Mark 13:2-4) shows otherwise.[1]

? Can you recall when you first realized Jesus was Deity, without beginning or end? How well do you understand that concept now? Explain. How should that understanding affect your walk with him? How has it affected you?

> *[9]I, John, your brother and companion in the suffering and kingdom and patient endurance that are ours in Jesus, was on the island of Patmos because of the word of God and the testimony of Jesus. [10]On the Lord's Day I was in the Spirit, and I heard behind me a loud voice like a trumpet, [11]which said: "Write on a scroll what you see and send it to the seven churches: to Ephesus, Smyrna, Pergamum, Thyatira, Sardis, Philadelphia and Laodicea."*

John wanted his readers to know that he was more than empathic, more than sympathetic, with them in their time of suffering—he was a companion of theirs in the kingdom and in the suffering which now accompanied such membership. He was banished to Patmos because he spoke the word of God as well as lived it. Living among non-Christians as a good moral "example" of Biblical values may make others uncomfortable in their sins, but intense persecution seldom comes until we follow Paul's admonition in Ephesians 5:11: "Have nothing to do with the fruitless deeds of darkness, but rather expose them." Since John was writing to the persecuted, they obviously were following Paul's directive. No one can accurately call himself a disciple without doing the same.

In 1:10, the mention of the Lord's Day is a reference to the first day of the week, our Sunday. This emphasis comes as no surprise, since the first day of the week had such preeminence in the New Testament. Jesus arose from the dead on the first day of the week (Mark 16:1-9). Jesus first appeared to his group of disciples on the first day of the week (John 20:19), and his next appearance to them was one week later, also on the first day of the week (John 20:26). The church was established on the Day of Pentecost, which always fell on the first day of the week. Acts 20:7 and 1 Corinthians 16:2 show that the key assembly for the early church was unquestionably on the first day of the week. Therefore, if all of the earth-shaking events of the new covenant had already occurred on this day of the week, it is only fitting that the apostle John should be in the Spirit on that day as he received the final revelation of God's will from the Lord Jesus Christ!

> *[12]I turned around to see the voice that was speaking to me. And when I turned I saw seven golden lampstands, [13]and among the lampstands was someone "like a son of man," dressed in a robe reaching down to his feet and with a golden sash around his chest. [14]His head and hair were white like wool, as white as snow, and his eyes were like blazing fire. [15]His feet were like bronze glowing in a furnace, and his voice was like the sound of rushing waters. [16]In his right hand he held seven stars, and out of his mouth came a sharp double-edged sword. His face was like the sun shining in all its brilliance.*
>
> *[17]When I saw him, I fell at his feet as though dead. Then he placed his right hand on me and said: "Do not be afraid. I am the First and the Last. [18]I am the Living One; I was dead, and behold I am alive for ever and ever! And I hold the keys of death and Hades.*
>
> *[19]"Write, therefore, what you have seen, what is now and what will take place later. [20]The mystery of the seven stars that you saw in my right hand and of the seven golden lampstands is this: The seven stars are the angels of the seven churches, and the seven lampstands are the seven churches."*

The remainder of the chapter is designed to portray Jesus in all his glory, thereby inspiring confidence in those who were experiencing, or about to experience, severe persecution. The voice as a trumpet (signifying a loud and clear message) causes John to turn and to see a vision of Jesus in the midst of seven golden lampstands. In the OT tabernacle, one lampstand with seven lamps was located in the temple's Holy Place. In John's vision, seven lampstands signified the seven churches to whom he was to write (1:20). Jesus in the center of them shows that he indeed is the head of the Body, leading and nourishing it. Since the purpose of a lampstand was to provide light, a church who has lost its mission of spreading light has lost its reason for existing and will be removed (2:4-5).

The dress of Jesus in this vision (1:13-16) shows his exaltation, as in the case of the angels in 15:6. His white head and hair are reminiscent of "the Ancient of Days" described in Daniel 7:9, suggesting the idea of purity, and probably maturity and wisdom. His blazing eyes are able to see everything at once, including the very thoughts and motives of men (1 Corinthians 4:5, Hebrews 4:13) and the plight of his children who are in trouble. Note the similarity of this portrayal of Jesus to a portrayal in Daniel 10:4-11 which produced the same reaction in both prophets who received the vision: They were absolutely *overwhelmed*—they fell to the ground as though dead or in a coma!

The double-edged sword coming out of Jesus' mouth (1:16) shows his absolute authority and the power of the word of God (Hebrews 4:12). In Revelation, it is used in judgment against both the world (19:15, 21) and the church (2:12, 16).

In view of Jesus' power, men who love him should take heart and not be filled with fear in his presence. After all, perfect love does drive out fear even of the Day of Judgment (1 John 4:17-18). Since he died and rose again, he has demonstrated his control over death and Hades (the unseen spirit world of the dead). Paul put the same idea in these words in Romans 14:8-9:

> *If we live, we live to the Lord; and if we die, we die to the Lord. So, whether we live or die, we belong to the Lord.*
> *For this very reason, Christ died and returned to life so that he might be the Lord of both the dead and the living.*

Now that John has seen this vision of his Lord (1:13-16) and has had his fears allayed, his specific commission to write now comes. When you see Jesus, you see God, and God can deal with all of man's problems.

In 1:20, the lampstands are identified as the seven churches and the stars as the angels of the churches. While several interpretations of the identity of the angels have been proposed by different commentators, most likely the angels represent the spiritual life of these churches. Note that 2:1 addresses the first letter to the "angel" of the church in Ephesus, and then 2:7 speaks of the "churches" listening to the Spirit's message.

From this point forward, since Christ in all his glory had been seen and John was prepared to receive the message, he turns his attention to the specific letters to these seven churches.

? Now that you have studied the first two chapters of the book, how are you feeling about studying Revelation? What is the most surprising lesson you have learned thus far? What have you learned that has made the greatest impact on your heart?

3

▼

Christ's Challenges to Seven Churches
Part 1
REVELATION 2

The brief letters to the seven churches follow a common outline. First, they are all dictated by the Lord. Second, they are all addressed to the "angel" of the church. Third, all have titles drawn from the visions given in Revelation 1. Fourth, they all have the same basic components and structure:

1. A greeting, often called a "salutation."
2. A description of Jesus, taken mostly from chapter one.
3. A commendation for the good things in the church (with the exception of Sardis and Laodicea).
4. A condemnation of the bad things in the church (with the exception of Smyrna and Philadelphia).
5. An appeal and warning.
6. An exhortation and a promise.

The Letter to the Church at Ephesus (2:1-7)

2:1 "To the angel of the church in Ephesus write:

These are the words of him who holds the seven stars in his right hand and walks among the seven golden lampstands: 2I know your deeds, your hard work and your perseverance. I know that you cannot tolerate wicked men, that you have tested those who claim to be apostles but are not, and have found them false. 3You have persevered and have endured hardships for my name, and have not grown weary.

4Yet I hold this against you: You have forsaken your first love. 5Remember the height from which you have fallen! Repent and do the things you did at first. If you do not repent, I will come to you and remove your lampstand from its place.

⁶But you have this in your favor: You hate the practices of the Nicolaitans, which I also hate.

⁷He who has an ear, let him hear what the Spirit says to the churches. To him who overcomes, I will give the right to eat from the tree of life, which is in the paradise of God."

The City

Ephesus was a powerful city in Asia Minor due to its commercial and religious importance. On Paul's third missionary journey, he established the church there by converting a dozen men each with a Jewish background (Acts 19:1-7). Further reading shows how Paul's work in Ephesus spread to all of Asia so that Luke could write that "all the Jews and Greeks who lived in the province of Asia heard the word of the Lord" (Acts 19:10). It was what we often call a "pillar" city, in that it exerted influence over a much larger region. Therefore, the early missionaries used such cities to form a strong church as a base of evangelistic operations for the spread of the Gospel to outlying areas. The other churches in Asia Minor most likely traced their roots back to the early work done in Ephesus. Two other notable "pillar" churches described in the New Testament are Jerusalem and Antioch. It is remarkable how few modern religious movements have followed this proven plan of evangelism.

The pride of the city of Ephesus was the temple of Artemis (called the temple of Diana by the Romans), one of the seven wonders of the ancient world. It was a huge ornate structure with over a hundred pillars donated by different kings from all over the world.[1] In spite of centuries of influence by the temple of Artemis, Paul faced this false religion head-on with amazing results!

About that time there arose a great disturbance about the Way. A silversmith named Demetrius, who made silver shrines of Artemis, brought in no little business for the craftsmen. He called them together, along with the workmen in related trades, and said: "Men, you know we receive a good income from this business. And you see and hear how this fellow Paul has convinced and led astray large numbers of people here in Ephesus and in practically the whole province of Asia. He says that man-made gods are no gods at all. There is danger not only that our trade will lose its good name, but also that the temple of the great goddess Artemis will be discredited, and the goddess herself, who is worshipped throughout the province of Asia and the world, will be robbed of her divine majesty." (Acts 19:23-27)

The verses following these describe a mob scene with the crowd yelling at the top of their lungs for two hours! Paul's courage to stand up publicly for his convictions led to the conversion of idolaters all over Asia to the consternation of those who did not obey his message.

The Church

The description of Jesus in the letter to the church at Ephesus is a combination of elements taken from 1:12-13, 16, 20. As he begins his review of the church, he commends them for several things: their hard work, perseverance, rejection of false teachers, endurance of hardships and hatred of evil practices. The original recipients of the letter were no doubt feeling great as the praise was read aloud at a church service. Their positive qualities were outstanding. Perseverance is an absolutely vital ingredient for personal growth (Romans 5:3-5, James 1:2-4), to say nothing of its essential role in keeping us faithful for a lifetime.

Were you surprised to see "hate" listed in the positive category (2:6)?

If we are to be imitators of God, we must love what he loves and hate what he hates. The denominational, worldly view of God tolerating or accepting almost anything and nearly everybody is decidedly false. A concordance study of God's hatred is eye opening and sobering. We normally explain that he hates sin and not the sinner, and in a practical sense, this explanation is true. However, our own tendency toward sentimentality must be tempered by such verses as these: "The arrogant cannot stand in your presence; you hate all who do wrong" (Psalm 5:5). "The LORD examines the righteous, but the wicked and those who love violence his soul hates" (Psalm 11:5). Suffice it to say that we cannot take any sin lightly!

As Jesus begins his criticisms of the Ephesian church, we see that the scope of his *commendations* does not lead to a watering down of the *condemnations*! These disciples were strong in doctrine but weak in love; orthodox in beliefs but unrighteous in the application of the greatest commands—to love God and to love their neighbors (Matthew 22:36-40). They had lost their "first love." What was that first love? It was their enthusiastic appreciative devotion they had as new converts. They had understood the magnitude of their sin and of God's love in the cross at the same time. Such an understanding surely had filled them with kingdom dreams and a willingness to go anywhere, do anything and give up everything! But time had taken its toll. They had cooled off gradually and perhaps almost imperceptibly, but the results were unmistakable. And now Jesus warns them to repent or perish (2:5).

Relationships are designed to grow. My relationship with my wife over the last 31 years has grown remarkably. However, we have paid the price to see it grow because we both have observed that most marriages level off and stagnate into mediocrity or deteriorate into divorce. Similarly, a disciple's relationship with God will follow exactly the same course unless he keeps daily fanning the flames of love and appreciation for God. It will not happen without paying the price of cultivating the relationship through listening to him speak to us in his word and speaking to him through prayer. Too few talk to him in a relational manner. Just think of how we build deep relationships with people. Among other things, we need time working together, playing together and sharing our feelings together in a vulnerable fashion. Why not do the same with God? Without developing these emotional bonds, we may persevere in religious activities without pleasing God. Cooling down in our "first love" devotion to God seems all too normal and acceptable to us because we have allowed Satan to deceive us. In the eyes of Jesus, the height of such falling is *monumental!*

The appeal in this letter is to remember, repent and do what they did as new converts with the same heart (2:5). The warning was that Jesus would remove their lampstand unless they heeded the appeal (also 2:5)! Since the lampstand signifies the church (1:20), this scripture shows that a group of people can lose their identity in God's sight as a true church. In the eyes of men they may be judged as quite acceptable, but God is the only Judge who matters! The precious promise to this church was clearly conditional, based on their repentance. From paradise lost in Genesis 3:22-24, we can now have paradise regained only through Jesus Christ and a zealous love for him (2:7).

? What in the letter to Ephesus do you most need in your life right now? As you studied, did you learn anything new about God? Sin? Yourself?

The Letter to the Church at Smyrna (2:8-11)

> [8] *"To the angel of the church in Smyrna write:*
> *These are the words of him who is the First and the Last, who died and came to life again. [9]I know your afflictions and your poverty—yet you are rich! I know the slander of those who say they are Jews and are not, but are a synagogue of Satan. [10]Do not be afraid of what you are about to suffer. I tell you, the devil will put some of you in prison to test you, and you will suffer persecution for ten days. Be faithful, even to the point of death, and I will give you the crown of life.*
> *[11]He who has an ear, let him hear what the Spirit says to the churches. He who overcomes will not be hurt at all by the second death."*

The City

The proud inhabitants of Smyrna believed themselves to be citizens of the "fairest city of Ionia." Located about thirty-five miles from Ephesus, the city was also a great trade center with a beautiful harbor. In fact, it was a model of a planned city with its wide streets, stately buildings and famous temples. No wonder Smyrna called itself the "Glory of Asia."

But Smyrna had more to "commend" it than beauty—it was intensely loyal to the Roman Empire and its emperors. Around 195 BC, a shrine to Roma, the goddess Rome, was erected and during the reign of Tiberias (14-37 AD), the city was chosen as the site of a temple dedicated to him. This temple joined a number of others, including those of Zeus and Aphrodite. This city was a veritable center of paganism. In addition, Smyrna was also home to a large Jewish population.

The Church

The description of Jesus in 2:8 comes from 1:17-18. He encourages the disciples in this vain city by telling them that he is aware of their afflictions and their poverty and reminds them that they are actually rich in his sight. True riches have nothing to do with material possessions or ease of life-style. This truth is easily stated but grasped emotionally only with great difficulty when we are facing tough times physically. Although material things are not wrong per se, Satan knows how to use our tendencies toward materialism to his advantage. As Paul put it, "For the love of money is a root of all kinds of evil. Some people, eager for money, have wandered from the faith and pierced themselves with many griefs" (1 Timothy 6:10).

Jesus has no disparaging words for this church, which must have brought much comfort to them when they first heard the words read (especially after hearing the rebuke received by their sister congregation in Ephesus!). Opposition has a way of helping disciples keep a right perspective about values, and in Smyrna the Jews were evidently the major opponents. Jesus' comments here should lay to rest the modern view that Israel still has a special place in the future plans of God. The gospel today is for the Jew as well as the Gentile, but Jews who reject Christ are under the control of Satan, not God. They have relinquished their claim to be the children of Abraham, for that designation now belongs to those who have been baptized into Christ (Romans 2:28-29, Galatians 3:27-29). Disciples of Jesus are now the only true people of God.

The Jews described in the letter to Smyrna likely had a sign above their synagogue door reading: "Synagogue of the LORD." However, Jesus gave it another name: "Synagogue of Satan"—a sharp reminder that what is highly valuable among men is often detestable in God's sight (Luke 16:15).

Obedience to the teachings of 2:10 requires deep convictions about life and death, heaven and hell. When we have the big-picture view of life in this world we see how fleeting it is and how significant eternity must be. Paul, who had seen the *other side* (2 Corinthians 12:2-10), had his perspective altered in a profound way. Read his words in 2 Corinthians 4:16-18 carefully.

> *Therefore we do not lose heart. Though outwardly we are*
> *wasting away, yet inwardly we are being renewed day by day.*
> *For our light and momentary troubles are achieving for us an*

eternal glory that far outweighs them all. So we fix our eyes not on what is seen, but on what is unseen. For what is seen is temporary, but what is unseen is eternal.

With this kind of understanding, we can deal successfully with our natural fears as persecution brings us to the point of death. (The "ten days" here (2:10) should not be taken as literal, but symbolic of a definite period, and most likely short.) Those who remain faithful must face the first death (physical), but not the second death (spiritual separation from God in eternity—see 21:8). As Jesus worded it in Matthew 10:28, "Do not be afraid of those who kill the body but cannot kill the soul. Rather, be afraid of the One who can destroy both soul and body in hell."

? Do you have fears about suffering for the cause of God's kingdom? Disciples in our day have been imprisoned for their faith. How does that affect you?

The Letter to the Church at Pergamum (2:12-17)

12 "To the angel of the church in Pergamum write:

These are the words of him who has the sharp, double-edged sword. 13 I know where you live—where Satan has his throne. Yet you remain true to my name. You did not renounce your faith in me, even in the days of Antipas, my faithful witness, who was put to death in your city—where Satan lives.

14 Nevertheless, I have a few things against you: You have people there who hold to the teaching of Balaam, who taught Balak to entice the Israelites to sin by eating food sacrificed to idols and by committing sexual immorality. 15 Likewise you also have those who hold to the teaching of the Nicolaitans. 16 Repent therefore! Otherwise, I will soon come to you and will fight against them with the sword of my mouth.

17 He who has an ear, let him hear what the Spirit says to the churches. To him who overcomes, I will give some of the hidden manna. I will also give him a white stone with a new name written on it, known only to him who receives it."

The City

Pergamum was located about thirty miles north of Smyrna and about fifteen miles inland from the Aegean Sea. It was a very important city, having served as the capital of the

province of Asia for more than two centuries. It was a center
of pagan religion, with temples to Zeus, Dionysus, Athena,
and Asklepios (the god of healing, signified by a snake—as
may be seen today in the traditional medical emblem). Several temples were erected to the Imperial Cult, deifying the
empire and its emperors. (Surely to the Christian, Satan had a
number of thrones in Pergamum; see Revelation 2:12-13).

A well known library housing 200,000 volumes was located there, second only to the library in Alexandria, Egypt.
When the king of Pergamum tried to hire the famous librar-
ian of Alexandria, the Egyptian king retaliated by cutting off
the supply of papyrus to Asia. As a result, parchment
(*pergamena* in Latin) was developed and the use of animal
skins as writing material thus came into common use.[2]

The Church

Jesus speaks to the church with his sharp, double-edged
sword (1:16) which cuts to the heart of the real issues and to
the innermost part of man's soul (Hebrews 4:12-13). As a gov-
ernmental authority, Rome had the right to bear the sword
(Romans 13:4), but in competition with Jesus for worship and
exaltation, she would learn who carried the more powerful
sword! The Empire eventually required citizens to burn a pinch
of incense on an altar to the Emperor and confess Caesar as
Lord. Those who refused would be denied jobs (13:16-17) or
killed like Antipas (2:13). The church at Pergamum was commended by the true Lord for not cowering in the face of such
intense persecution.

However, the sword of the Lord cut both ways, as commendation of faithfulness was followed by condemnation of
sin. Some in the church had accepted the teachings of Balaam
and the Nicolaitans. Since Balaam, a prophet of God, had been
unable to directly curse the Israelites in the Old Testament,
he counseled King Balak to lead them into compromise, resulting in idolatry and immorality (Numbers 22-25). In the
first century, the pagan temples were always alluring to those
disciples who were trying to fit in and not be seen as radically
different from those around them. Christians cannot "blend
in" because oil and water cannot mix, nor can light and darkness cohabit! Seemingly small compromises lead to larger ones,

until finally the most ungodly lines are crossed. In the name of evangelism, we are to become all things to all men in order to reach as many as possible (1 Corinthians 9:19-27), but the last verse in that passage makes it clear that the "all things" does not include self-indulgence! "No, I beat my body and make it my slave so that after I have preached to others, I myself will not be disqualified for the prize."

The identity of the Nicolaitans in 2:15 is uncertain. We know that the Ephesian disciples were commended for hating their practices (2:6), in sharp contrast to the disciples at Pergamum! The teachings under question seemed to be related to those described in 2:14, suggesting some form of worldliness and compromise. We are *in* the world to influence the world, but we cannot be *of* it in any way. After a call to repent, Jesus threatens to fight against *them*, meaning those in the church who did not repent (2:16).

Those who did respond properly were promised hidden manna and a white stone inscribed with a new name understood only by its recipients (2:17). The new name was the name of Christ himself (3:12). God's word is written in such a way as to reveal hearts. Readers with a desire to see will see its spiritual truths and those with worldly hearts will not see it (Romans 8:5-8, 1 Corinthians 2:12-14). White is the color of victory and purity, and the reference to a white stone may trace back to the use of white and black stones in ancient law to show guilt or innocence. Hence, for the Christian who heard and responded to Jesus' teachings, the stone signified their acquittal.

? The concept of "hating" sin was mentioned again. What is good about hating? What is bad about it? As you examine your own heart, how have you hated in a right way and in a wrong way?

The Letter to the Church at Thyatira (2:18-29)

> [18] *"To the angel of the church in Thyatira write:*
>
> *These are the words of the Son of God, whose eyes are like blazing fire and whose feet are like burnished bronze.* [19] *I know your deeds, your love and faith, your service and perseverance, and that you are now doing more than you did at first.*
>
> [20] *Nevertheless, I have this against you: You tolerate that woman Jezebel, who calls herself a prophetess. By her teaching she misleads my servants into sexual immorality and the*

eating of food sacrificed to idols. [21]*I have given her time to repent of her immorality, but she is unwilling.* [22]*So I will cast her on a bed of suffering, and I will make those who commit adultery with her suffer intensely, unless they repent of her ways.* [23]*I will strike her children dead. Then all the churches will know that I am he who searches hearts and minds, and I will repay each of you according to your deeds.* [24]*Now I say to the rest of you in Thyatira, to you who do not hold to her teaching and have not learned Satan's so-called deep secrets (I will not impose any other burden on you):* [25]*Only hold on to what you have until I come.*

[26]*To him who overcomes and does my will to the end, I will give authority over the nations—*

[27]*'He will rule them with an iron scepter;*
he will dash them to pieces like pottery'—

just as I have received authority from my Father. [28]*I will also give him the morning star.* [29]*He who has an ear, let him hear what the Spirit says to the churches."*

The City

Thyatira was a wealthy city, located about forty miles southeast of Pergamum nearly midway between it and Sardis. As could be inferred from the account in Acts 16 regarding Lydia, the city was noted for its purple dyes and dyed garments. This color of royalty came from the madder root and from the throat of the shellfish *murex*. The actual color may have been closer to what we normally call red, but it was a highly valued dye to be sure.

The city was also known for its trade guilds (unions), which form the backdrop for many of the challenges faced by the church there. The union meetings took place in the pagan temples and were associated with sacrifices to the pagan gods or goddesses. Literal sexual immorality was often a part of the worship of fertility goddesses. Therefore, eating food sacrificed to idols and immorality in this setting were closely connected with supposed business meetings in the temples.

The Church

The description of Jesus (from 1:14-15) shows his indignation with the sins he saw in the church. His eyes were flashing with righteous anger and his feet were ready to trample those who persisted in sin even after his warning. Verse 19 shows that they were not without good deeds, and for those, they were commended. But it is clear that Jesus is dealing with a church within a church—a righteous group who refused to compromise and another group who majored in rationalizations. However, even in the case of those not personally involved in the compromises, they were tolerating what was practiced instead of directly dealing with the sins of their brothers and sisters.

Most religious groups today have no idea of what their members are doing, and when they inadvertently find out, they look the other way in order not to "meddle" in another's "private" affairs. What a sad commentary on the state of religion set adrift from its Biblical moorings! And what a sad commentary on the state of any individual disciple who does not consider himself his brother's keeper! Even if we are not involved personally in a certain sin, our failure to confront the sin in other disciples makes us guilty as an accomplice.

"Jezebel" (most certainly, not her real name) was evidently an outspoken woman in the church wielding a powerful influence. Sexual references in this passage appear to be mixed, in that both physical and spiritual immorality are in view. Old Testament and New Testament both designate spiritual unfaithfulness as immorality. Such strong language has its basis in God's view of his people's covenant relationship with him as a marriage. (See Hosea 2, Isaiah 54:5, and Jeremiah 2:2, 3:14, 31:32 for this common analogy in the Old Testament.) In the NT relationship, the church is considered the bride of Christ (2 Corinthians 11:2, Ephesians 5:23-32, Revelation 21:1-9). On our part, loving the world thus causes God to make this pronouncement:

> *You adulterous people, don't you know that friendship with the world is hatred toward God? Anyone who chooses to be a friend of the world becomes an enemy of God. (James 4:4)*

Therefore, the immorality mentioned in 2:20, because of its connection with eating meat sacrificed to idols, was probably literal. In 2:21-22, the adultery is likely spiritual on the part of "Jezebel" and the ones who succumbed to her influence. Specifically, she was most likely arguing for compromises in connection with the trade union meetings and the practices associated with them in the pagan temples. It would have been easy for disciples to make concessions in an effort to keep their jobs and to thus provide for their families. But sin is sin, no matter how logical the rationalization may seem when filtered through our own self-serving, self-protecting viewpoints. God will not be fooled and he will not be sentimental when calling such sin into account (2:22-23).

Note the Gnostic background in 2:24. Gnosticism (from the Greek word *gnosis*, meaning "knowledge") was based on the belief that material things are evil; those of this persuasion were either *libertines* or *ascetics*. Ascetics took the route of self-denial to an ungodly extreme by refusing anything which might be pleasurable. In 1 Timothy 4:1-3 and Colossians 2:20-23, asceticism is plainly condemned. On the other hand, libertines claimed that since the flesh was inherently evil, actions were inconsequential—as long as the right knowledge was present, moral behavior mattered little. 2 Peter 2 describes this type of gnosticism, as does our present passage in Revelation 2.

 Gnostics, especially of the libertine persuasion, believed themselves to have a deeper understanding of God's will than seemed apparent on the printed page. No matter what the Scriptures *seemed* to say (to the uninformed commoner), they felt they could read between the lines to see what was *really* meant! To say that they were dangerous is to understate the case considerably. However, God cuts to the heart of the matter and calls this Jezebel's teaching Satanic. She claimed that her doctrine of worldly compromise was based on the "deep secrets of God," but in truth, her teachings were nothing more than the "deep secrets of Satan!"

In 2:24, those who reject Jezebel's teaching and remain faithful will share in the authority of Christ, for they are royal seed (2:26-27). This rule is not in some future millennial kingdom—it is enjoyed in this life when we are Christ's. Ephesians 2:6-7a says:

> *And God raised us up with Christ and seated us with him in the heavenly realms in Christ Jesus, in order that in the coming ages he might show the incomparable riches of his grace....*

And Romans 5:17 states that "those who receive God's abundant provision of grace and of the gift of righteousness reign in life through the one man, Jesus Christ." The bright morning star is also promised to the faithful, which is the anticipation of a new day of victory from the bright Morning Star himself (22:16).

? The tendency to compromise is shown in the church at Thyatira. What are your main temptations to compromise? What can you do to avoid compromising in these areas?

4

▼

Christ's Challenges to Seven Churches
Part 2
REVELATION 3

As we continue reading the letters to the seven churches, we see the significant differences in these congregations. Some had nothing bad said about them, some had nothing good said about them, and some had both good and bad in their descriptions. One lesson is often overlooked in studying these churches, namely that each had its own personality. Even though the types of individual disciples may have been varied, the overall personality could be identified. This fact shows us that newer disciples tend strongly to take on the characteristics of the majority in the group, for that majority determines the overall personality. The challenge comes in setting the right standards and then expecting the new disciples to imitate the more mature.

What is your church like as a group? How would you describe its personality? If everyone in your congregation were like you, how would Jesus describe the group? Those are the kinds of questions we must ask and answer about our personal lives and about our churches. Discipleship works—for good or for bad. Notice the personalities of these final three churches.

The Letter to the Church at Sardis (3:1-6)

> *3:1 "To the angel of the church in Sardis write:*
> *These are the words of him who holds the seven spirits of God and the seven stars. I know your deeds; you have a reputation of being alive, but you are dead. ²Wake up! Strengthen what remains and is about to die, for I have not found your deeds complete in the sight of my God. ³Remember, therefore, what you have received and heard; obey it, and repent. But if*

*you do not wake up, I will come like a thief, and you will not
know at what time I will come to you.*

*⁴Yet you have a few people in Sardis who have not soiled
their clothes. They will walk with me, dressed in white, for
they are worthy. ⁵He who overcomes will, like them, be dressed
in white. I will never blot out his name from the book of life,
but will acknowledge his name before my Father and his angels. ⁶He who has an ear, let him hear what the Spirit says to
the churches."*

The City

Sardis, located about thirty miles from Thyatira, was one
of the oldest and most famous cities in Asia Minor. Located
on a smooth rock hill that was extremely steep, the city had a
location that nearly defied assault. Yet, it had fallen twice
due to carelessness and lack of vigilance, once in 549 BC to
Cyrus, king of Persia, and again in 218 BC to Antiochus the
Great. Therefore, the admonition to "wake up" in 3:2-3 had
historical significance.

The people of Sardis were known to be wealthy pleasure
seekers with little purpose other than self-indulgence. Regret-
tably, the church in the city had succumbed to much the same
mind-set. Nothing is mentioned about persecution in the letter, which may account for the false sense of security felt by
the complacent disciples.

The Church

This church received practically no commendation, except
for the mention of a few who had not followed the majority
into sin. But they were not praised for any specifics beyond their
refusal to follow the crowd. As a whole, the church was amazingly deceived. They had a good reputation among sister congregations, but were, in fact, *dead*! Just as a person can be dead
while living (1 Timothy 5:6), so can a church. What shock must
have permeated the crowd as the congregational leader first read
this letter to them! Men tend to judge the condition of churches
and disciples from a physical perspective, but God is not fooled.
He is a reader of minds and an evaluator of motives.

No specific sins of the church are mentioned. Their chief
sin was in doing few or no positive deeds. Being a disciple is

much more than the avoidance of sin. We will be judged mainly by what we do, not by what we refuse to do. Jesus spoke to those of his day about cleaning their house but leaving it empty, thus allowing Satan to reenter them with even more demons (Matthew 12:43-45). If we are not focused on imitating the character and mission of Jesus, we are none of his! The disciples at Sardis had been better at beginning projects than finishing them. God demands that we both talk the talk and walk the walk. Truly, "The way to hell is paved with good intentions."

Just as their city had been destroyed twice by failing to watch the enemy, the Christians were well on their way to spiritual destruction due to complacency, thus the admonition to wake up, remember, obey and repent. Otherwise, they would be destroyed by Jesus coming like a thief in the night (a metaphor normally used in reference to the destruction of non-Christians; see 1 Thessalonians 5:1-4). In spite of the sad condition of the church in general, a few people had remained righteous. Being in a group that is sinful does not make everyone sinful, and conversely, being in a group that is righteous does not make everyone righteous. The question is not how the church is doing; the real question is how are *you* doing? Judgment Day is an individual matter, not a group matter. The ones in Sardis who did not repent would be blotted out of the book of life (a designation used six times in Revelation but only two more times in the rest of the Bible). The book of life is not a literal book, but its mention reinforces the fact that God knows those who are his (2 Timothy 2:19). Obviously, neither John nor Jesus were advocates of the now widely popular doctrine of "once saved, always saved"!

Notice the promise in 3:5 to acknowledge the names of the overcomers to the Father and his angels. The wording of the promise is based on a combination of Matthew 10:32 and Luke 12:8. In the context of these passages, having our name acknowledged is based on our acknowledgment of the name of Jesus in sharing our faith boldly and fearlessly. Therefore, a major part of overcoming is staying focused on the mission of Jesus to seek and to save the lost! Can anyone doubt that the heart of following him is to follow him in this mission? Had the first century church *not* been thus focused, the persecution would never have raged as it did.

? Have you ever been seriously deceived about where you were spiritually, thinking that you were doing much better than you actually were? How did it make you feel when you discovered that this was the case? What are you doing to make sure it doesn't happen again?

The Letter to the Church at Philadelphia (3:7-13)

> [7]*"To the angel of the church in Philadelphia write:*
> *These are the words of him who is holy and true, who holds the key of David. What he opens no one can shut, and what he shuts no one can open.* [8]*I know your deeds. See, I have placed before you an open door that no one can shut. I know that you have little strength, yet you have kept my word and have not denied my name.* [9]*I will make those who are of the synagogue of Satan, who claim to be Jews though they are not, but are liars—I will make them come and fall down at your feet and acknowledge that I have loved you.* [10]*Since you have kept my command to endure patiently, I will also keep you from the hour of trial that is going to come upon the whole world to test those who live on the earth.*
> [11]*I am coming soon. Hold on to what you have, so that no one will take your crown.* [12]*Him who overcomes I will make a pillar in the temple of my God. Never again will he leave it. I will write on him the name of my God and the name of the city of my God, the new Jerusalem, which is coming down out of heaven from my God; and I will also write on him my new name.* [13]*He who has an ear, let him hear what the Spirit says to the churches."*

The City

Philadelphia was founded by King Attalus II, called *Philadelphus* (brother lover) in about 150 BC because of his devotion to his brother and predecessor Ecumenes II. The city was located about thirty miles southeast of Sardis, and had been built as the gateway to the East to spread the Greek culture. It became an important and wealthy trade center. The surrounding countryside yielded excellent grapes, which led to the worship of Dionysus, the Greek god of wine, becoming preeminent in Philadelphia. However, a number of temples dedicated to the worship of other pagan deities could be found in the city. Also, a significant Jewish population contributed to the persecution of Christians.

In 17 AD, a major earthquake destroyed a dozen cities in the area, including both Sardis and Philadelphia. The emperor Tiberius provided funds from the national treasury to rebuild these cities. Out of appreciation, the city's name was changed to Neocaesarea (New Caesar), which is alluded to in 3:12. Because of the frequent tremors felt in the area for years, many residents of Philadelphia lived outside the main city in make-shift quarters.

The Church

The description of Christ in 3:7 introduces figures not found in Revelation 1. Jesus has the key of David, by which he determines who is really in his kingdom: those who worship him rather than the Jews who claimed the ancient relationship with David.

The open door was promised by Jesus to all who would knock faithfully (Matthew 7:7-8). In Paul's writing, the open door was an open door for evangelism (1 Corinthians 16:9, 2 Corinthians 2:12, Colossians 4:3). Even though the church in Philadelphia had little strength (perhaps due to size), they were carrying out the mission. Nothing negative was said about them. The presence of persecution makes it clear that they were not simply "holding their own." In 3:8, keeping Jesus' word is inseparably connected with not denying his name. Again, in Matthew 10:26-33, the denial of Jesus is equated with failing to verbally share our faith.

As in Smyrna, Philadelphia had a synagogue of Jews which God recognized as a synagogue of Satan. True Jews are not fleshly ones but spiritual ones (Christians). Actually, this had been true even during the OT period. Only a remnant of Jewish people had been people of faith. God used the nation of Israel as a vital part of his plan to prepare for the coming of Christ and the spread of the gospel to all people. They were an elect nation for these purposes, but they were not right with God merely because of this election. In fact, there were two concurrent elections taking place during this period. One was the national election as noted above and the other was an individual spiritual election. No one was a part of the latter without faith. Most Jews were confused on this point, thinking themselves to be right with God simply because they were in the ancestry of Abraham and a part of the chosen nation. The book of Romans, particularly chapters 9-11, makes this difference quite clear. Our present passage does the same.

In 3:10, the disciples in this city were promised some respite from the imminent spreading persecution. Either they would be spared the main brunt of it, or they were enabled to endure it with grace. (See 1 Corinthians 10:13 for the parameters of the trials God allows in the Christian's life.)

Several statements in the latter part of this letter reflect the background of Philadelphia. To be a pillar in God's temple reflects the practice in that city of erecting pillars to outstanding citizens. "Never again will he leave it" reflects the fear of earthquakes in that region which often led to the people running out of the city when the tremors started. The "new name" may reflect the renaming of their city to Neocaesarea, as mentioned above. Without question, patient endurance of difficult times for the sake of God would be rewarded in bountiful ways.

? By this point, the presence of serious persecution in this first century setting has become very obvious. How do you feel when someone persecutes you for your faith? How do you feel when negative charges are made against the church? Does it strengthen or weaken your faith?

The Letter to the Church at Laodicea (3:14-22)

[14] "To the angel of the church in Laodicea write:

These are the words of the Amen, the faithful and true witness, the ruler of God's creation. [15] I know your deeds, that you are neither cold nor hot. I wish you were either one or the other! [16] So, because you are lukewarm—neither hot nor cold— I am about to spit you out of my mouth. [17] You say, 'I am rich; I have acquired wealth and do not need a thing.' But you do not realize that you are wretched, pitiful, poor, blind and naked. [18] I counsel you to buy from me gold refined in the fire, so you can become rich; and white clothes to wear, so you can cover your shameful nakedness; and salve to put on your eyes, so you can see.

[19] Those whom I love I rebuke and discipline. So be earnest, and repent. [20] Here I am! I stand at the door and knock. If anyone hears my voice and opens the door, I will come in and eat with him, and he with me.

>   *²¹To him who overcomes, I will give the right to sit with me on my throne, just as I overcame and sat down with my Father on his throne. ²²He who has an ear, let him hear what the Spirit says to the churches."*

The City

Laodicea, located some ninety miles east of Ephesus and fifty miles southeast of Philadelphia, was a proud and powerful city. After being destroyed by an earthquake in 60 AD, its citizens refused financial aid from the empire, choosing rather to finance their own rebuilding.

Three primary commercial aspects of Laodicea brought the city to prominence. One, it was a center of banking, noted for being one of the wealthiest cities in the world. Two, it was an area of wool manufacture, producing a valuable black wool from a special breed of sheep. Three, a famous school of medicine was located just outside the city. The school developed an eye salve which was used widely. Each of these important financial aspects is reflected in the letter to them.

The Church

The church at Laodicea receives absolutely no commendation, but a strong censure for her sins. Her collective lukewarmness made Jesus *nauseous*! Our human nature tends to think that being somewhat warm toward Jesus is superior to being cold. Not so! Actually, the life of a lukewarm person has a much more damaging impact on others than does a cold person (a non-Christian). Hypocrisy is a terrible malady bringing terrible results. Jesus makes it clear that we will either be on fire with zeal for him or we will be lost. "Hot" in this passage comes from a word (*zestos*) which suggests reaching the boiling point. (See Acts 18:25 and Romans 12:11 for examples based on the same root word.) Jesus' teachings about discipleship in passages like Luke 9 and 14 were not unattainable ideals; they were principles upon which daily lives must be based. When these teachings are not reflected in the disciple's commitment level, Jesus spits (literally *vomits*) them out. Can there be any doubt that this means removing them from a saved relationship with him?

In the following verses, the lukewarmness of the Laodiceans is defined further. They were self-sufficient in their spiritual smugness. Like their fellow citizens, they believed they were rich. They did not see their desperate need for the grace of God. They interpreted physical benefits as proof that God was pleased with them. However, he saw them as utterly destitute. The gospel of "follow God and get rich" is not novel to our day. The Jews taught it, as did many others from all kinds of religious backgrounds. Jesus' personal life-style alone should annihilate this humanistic theory. All of us need to thoroughly examine our hearts regarding the role material possessions play in our view of having life "to the full" (John 10:10). My concern for disciples in first-world nations is that we may be closer to living like the Laodicean disciples than we think.

They needed the true gold of spiritual commitment to Christ, the white clothes cleansed by the blood of their Savior (7:14); and the eye salve of spiritual discernment to restore their vision. To receive these antidotes for their spiritual maladies, they had to be earnest ("zealous" in other versions) and repent. Jesus' love here is from *phileo* (the warm friendship type of love) rather than *agape* (the deeper commitment type of love). Although *agape* is most often used to describe God's love, the use of *phileo* shows Jesus' emotional attachment to us and how it hurts his heart when we allow our devotion for him to cool. But out of that love, he rebukes and chastens! True love cares enough to intervene. If we accept his loving discipline, we will respond to it without overreaction, neither taking it lightly nor being overwhelmed by it (Hebrews 12:5). And if we understand true love, we too will avoid showing sentimentality. Sentimental love is selfish, with a primary concern of how intervention might affect *us* if the one being rebuked responds poorly. Jesus was never sentimental with others, and we cannot be either.

He stands at the door of our hearts and seeks readmittance. Isn't that a sad picture? Jesus, the one who loves us enough to bear all of our sins on the cross is now shown pleading with us to let him back in. Three vital lessons must be learned from 3:20. One, the sin of lukewarmness is very serious. It puts Jesus out of our lives, which is another way of saying that those who persist in lukewarmness will lose their relationship with him. Two, we must open the door for him. He will not force it open. Holman Hunt painted a picture of Jesus knocking at our heart's door and showed only one door knob—the one on the inside which must be opened from within.[1] Three, Jesus loves us deeply enough to plead unashamedly for entrance back into our hearts and lives. When we do overcome our sins, we gain sweet fellowship with him and share in his throne.

Thus ends the letters to the seven churches. It is almost uncanny how closely the descriptions parallel the condition of churches in our day, and how desperately we need to heed the same warnings and admonitions given to them 1900 years ago. The more things change, the more they remain the same. Material conditions may vary in the extreme, but the hearts of men cry out for the same healing offered only by the Son of Man. Now on to visions of beasts, blood and glory!

? Do you think you see "lukewarmness" in the same way Jesus does? Explain. What will you do differently as a result of studying the messages to the seven churches of Asia?

5
▼

Mine Eyes Have Seen the Glory!
REVELATION 4 AND 5

As we begin reading Revelation 4, we see the type of writing for which the book is most known—one symbolic vision after another. Unlike the letters to the seven churches, which were easily read and understood, the remainder of Revelation is not so readily grasped. At this point, we will do well to let our imaginations be impressed with what amounts to a dramatic presentation. If we try to isolate and examine the specific images within the visions in great detail, we are bound to be sidetracked. They are intended to provide inspiration and excitement to our hearts much more than they are designed to provoke an intellectual bit-by-bit dissection. A literalistic approach to studying Revelation is certain to produce frustration and misunderstanding.

The flow of the book thus far is similar to Romans. In chapter one of both books, Jesus is introduced and we are reminded of our blessings in him. Then sin is confronted and convictions produced (in the good-hearted!) through chapter three. Once we have been properly convicted of sin, then and only then are we prepared to understand and receive grace. Chapter 4 in both books moves into this subject, although in very different formats. Regarding this progression, we are reminded of Jesus' words in John 16:7-8. Here Jesus promises to send the Holy Spirit to convict the world of sin, righteousness and judgment. Man cannot be convinced of grace until he is first convicted of sin.

Of God on His Throne (4:1-11)

⁴:¹After this I looked, and there before me was a door standing open in heaven. And the voice I had first heard speaking to me like a trumpet said, "Come up here, and I will show you what must take place after this." ²At once I was in the Spirit, and there before me was a throne in heaven with someone sitting on it. ³And the one who sat there had the appearance of jasper and carnelian. A rainbow, resembling an emerald, encircled the throne.

As the above scene unfolds before the eyes of John, he sees a door standing open in heaven. God is inviting him to see the visions, which will reveal future events. Compare this scene to Ezekiel's initial reception of his visions (Ezekiel 1). At once John was in the Spirit (prepared to receive the visions), and was ushered into heaven to see him who sat upon the throne. On earth, much attention was given to the one who sat on the throne of the Roman empire. In heaven, all attention is given to the One who rules heaven and earth. From man's vantage point, things may look bleak and uncontrollable, but from God's vantage point, everything is under his control and every situation is being woven into the fabric of his ultimate plan for the universe. The early Christians needed to lift their eyes up from the pains on earth to the joys of heaven. The real issue is never what is hurting us in the here and now; it is what will be our lot a hundred years from now, or a thousand years from now, or a million years from now! God reigns! Let's calm our hearts.

The figures in 4:3 may be designed solely to impress and excite. If meaning is to be attached to colors, for example, the jasper stone (white) was meant to convey God's holiness and righteousness, and the carnelian stone (red) his justice. The rainbow would likely have suggested the promises of a covenant-making God, as in Genesis 9:12-17 after the flood. As you can see, it simply is not possible to identify all of the specifics in each vision. Although we will make some attempt to suggest possibilities, the real focus of Revelation 4 is that God, not the egomaniac emperor Domitian, is in charge. We cannot allow ourselves to get caught up in details to the point that we miss the big picture in Revelation.

⁴Surrounding the throne were twenty-four other thrones, and seated on them were twenty-four elders. They were dressed in white and had crowns of gold on their heads. ⁵From the throne came flashes of lightning, rumblings and peals of thunder. Before the throne, seven lamps were blazing. These are the seven spirits of God. ⁶Also before the throne there was what looked like a sea of glass, clear as crystal.

> *In the center, around the throne, were four living creatures,*
> *and they were covered with eyes, in front and in back. [7]The first*
> *living creature was like a lion, the second was like an ox, the*
> *third had a face like a man, the fourth was like a flying eagle.*

Next, we are introduced to twenty-four elders sitting on thrones. The meaning of numbers is probably one of the most certain interpretation issues in the book. As noted earlier, "twelve" always symbolizes God's group or organization. The most plausible usage here is that all of the redeemed of the ages are represented by the OT twelve tribes and by the NT twelve apostles. The victory song in 15:2-4 is the song of Moses (OT) and the Lamb (NT). Jesus promised the apostles that they would "sit on twelve thrones, judging the twelve tribes of Israel" (Matthew 19:28). Therefore, as John looked at the throne of God, he saw proof that all who remain faithful to God would be with him, enjoying their rewards. They were dressed in white (signifying purity and victory) and wore crowns of gold. The crowns (*stephanos*) are those emphasizing victory, rather than simply ruling crowns ("diadems").

The figures of 4:5 are reminiscent of Exodus 19:16-19 when God's Spirit was blazing as he prepared to give the law at Mount Sinai. "Seven" (4:5) here signifies the Holy Spirit in his perfection as he illuminates through his inspired message.

The sea of glass in 4:6 likely is meant to suggest the transcendence of God, as he "lives in unapproachable light" (1 Timothy 6:16). Even as he wrote from Patmos, John was physically separated from the churches by the sea. In Revelation 21:1, when the present order of things has ended, "the first heaven and the first earth had passed away, and there was no longer any sea."

Four living creatures are introduced, which are intended to further emphasize the sovereign rule of Almighty God. A number of similarities exist between these creatures and those of Ezekiel 1, the seraphs of Isaiah 6:2-3 and the cherubim of Ezekiel 10. Trying to assign meanings to each feature of the creatures would be fruitless. However, what they symbolize as a whole is more important to understand. The two most reasonable ideas are that they represent all created life glorifying God, or that they are extensions of God, showing his attributes. The former seems most likely, because the creatures worship God day and night. If this view is correct, the lion could represent wild animals, the ox domestic animals, the man humans, and the eagle the bird kingdom. (Similarly, Psalm 148 is a good example of how the Bible depicts all of creation praising and glorifying its Creator.)

> *8Each of the four living creatures had six wings and was covered with eyes all around, even under his wings. Day and night they never stop saying:*
>
> *"Holy, holy, holy*
> *is the Lord God Almighty,*
> *who was, and is, and is to come."*
>
> *9Whenever the living creatures give glory, honor and thanks to him who sits on the throne and who lives for ever and ever, 10the twenty-four elders fall down before him who sits on the throne, and worship him who lives for ever and ever. They lay their crowns before the throne and say:*
>
> > *11"You are worthy, our Lord and God,*
> > *to receive glory and honor and power,*
> > *for you created all things,*
> > *and by your will they were created*
> > *and have their being."*

The majestic throne scene closes out with the twenty-four elders and the four living creatures praising God. By now, the original readers of Revelation are feeling relieved and inspired. Their eyes are far removed from the mundane affairs of life and even from the threats of physical persecution. God Almighty reigns, and all is well. Their eyes have seen his glory, they have breathed a sigh of relief, and now they eagerly await the description of the next vision.

? How has seeing God on his heavenly throne affected your view of problems? What in your life seems out of God's control? What will you do to get faith for that area of your life? Who can you talk to who has had a similar struggle?

Of the Worthy Lamb (5:1-14)

> *5:1Then I saw in the right hand of him who sat on the throne a scroll with writing on both sides and sealed with seven seals. 2And I saw a mighty angel proclaiming in a loud voice, "Who*

> is worthy to break the seals and open the scroll?" *³But no one
> in heaven or on earth or under the earth could open the scroll
> or even look inside it. ⁴I wept and wept because no one was
> found who was worthy to open the scroll or look inside. ⁵Then
> one of the elders said to me, "Do not weep! See, the Lion of
> the tribe of Judah, the Root of David, has triumphed. He is
> able to open the scroll and its seven seals."*

After having seen God on his throne, now the scene turns to Jesus, the original "Lion King." In John's gospel, he records Jesus saying, "Do not let your hearts be troubled. Trust in God; trust also in me" (John 14:1). The same order is found in Revelation 4 and 5—trust in God and his Son.

The scroll in God's hand was probably papyrus. The unusual thing about it was that it had writing on both sides, which shows the message to be a full one. (Compare to Ezekiel's scroll in Ezekiel 2:9-10.) The content of the message is then revealed in the visions of Revelation.

Further, it was sealed with seven (perfection) wax seals. But no one was found morally worthy to break the seals and open the scroll in order that the message might be read. John, realizing the tremendous importance of the message, weeps and weeps.

Then one of the elders informs John that the Christ can open the seals. If no one in heaven, on earth or under the earth was worthy to open the seals besides Jesus, then he must of necessity be Deity. Twice in Revelation, John fell down to worship an angel and was promptly forbidden to do such (19:10, 22:8-9). However, the angels worshipped Jesus, demonstrating his Deity. The Jehovah's Witnesses and others teach that Jesus is a created being, a ruling angel, which is absolute heresy. Note that Jesus is both Lion (5:5) and Lamb (5:6), ruler and sacrifice. (See Genesis 49:8-10 for Jacob's Messianic prophecy that a special ruler would arise from Judah's tribe.)

> *⁶Then I saw a Lamb, looking as if it had been slain, stand-
> ing in the center of the throne, encircled by the four living
> creatures and the elders. He had seven horns and seven eyes,
> which are the seven spirits of God sent out into all the earth.
> ⁷He came and took the scroll from the right hand of him who
> sat on the throne. ⁸And when he had taken it, the four living*

creatures and the twenty-four elders fell down before the Lamb.
Each one had a harp and they were holding golden bowls full
of incense, which are the prayers of the saints.

As John turns to see the Lion, he sees a Lamb. Just like
dreams change figures suddenly, so did this vision. The Lamb
is in the center of the throne, which he shares with his Father
(3:21). He had seven horns (perfect power) and seven eyes
(perfect knowledge through the Holy Spirit sent out into all
the earth). The Psalmist wrote: "Where can I go from your
Spirit? Where can I flee from your presence? If I go up to the
heavens, you are there; if I make my bed in the depths, you
are there" (Psalm 139:7-8).

In 5:7, the action of Jesus taking the scroll was a decisive
one. The Greek construction shows dramatic unhesitant action,
demonstrating the authority of Jesus and his intimacy with the
Father. As the triumphant Lion/Lamb, he had utmost confidence.
Therefore, we can have utmost confidence in him and his work
in our behalf. The heavenly beings now worship the confident
Lamb, spurred on by the prayers of the saints. (The portrayal of
prayers as incense is found in a number of passages, including
8:3-4.) Keep in mind that Biblically the word "saint" refers to
any and every Christian. In fact, the word is used in this manner more than forty times in the New Testament.

⁹And they sang a new song:

> *"You are worthy to take the scroll*
> *   and to open its seals,*
> *because you were slain,*
> *   and with your blood you purchased men for God*
> *   from every tribe and language and people and nation.*
> *¹⁰You have made them to be a kingdom and priests to serve*
> *   our God,*
> *   and they will reign on the earth."*
> *¹¹Then I looked and heard the voice of many angels, num-*
> *bering thousands upon thousands, and ten thousand times ten*
> *thousand. They encircled the throne and the living creatures*
> *and the elders. ¹²In a loud voice they sang:*

> *"Worthy is the Lamb, who was slain,*
> *to receive power and wealth and wisdom and strength*
> *and honor and glory and praise!"*

[13]Then I heard every creature in heaven and on earth and under the earth and on the sea, and all that is in them, singing:

"To him who sits on the throne and to the Lamb be praise and honor and glory and power, for ever and ever!"
[14]The four living creatures said, "Amen," and the elders fell down and worshiped.

The new song is new (*kainos*) in kind, not new from the standpoint of time. This new song of redemption is incomprehensible to non-Christians (14:3), because its truths are spiritually discerned (1 Corinthians 2:14). The word of the cross will remain foolishness to those who are perishing, but to the redeemed, it is the wisdom and the power of God (1 Corinthians 1:18-25). The song reveals the power of the cross in its purpose (saving men for God), its scope (men of all types), and its results (making us a kingdom and priests). The "reigning" in 5:10 is what we *are* now doing on the earth as priests (disciples), not what premillennialists say we *will* do.

The elders and living creatures are joined by myriads of angels in offering praise to the worthy Lamb. As the Hebrew writer gives us insight into what life in the kingdom is like, he draws a similar picture: "But you have come to Mount Zion, to the heavenly Jerusalem, the city of the living God. You have come to thousands upon thousands of angels in joyful assembly" (Hebrews 12:22). When the persecuted of the first century felt the impact of these visions, surely they followed the example of the four living creatures and elders in shouting "Amen!" and falling down to worship! (5:14). Once the human heart comprehends the Biblical portrayal of God in all his glory, the world rights itself and peace invades the soul. Those thus blessed could sing with fervor, "Mine eyes have seen his glory." May we join heaven and earth in falling to our knees before the One who sits on his throne and the Lamb whose blood has redeemed us! Mine eyes have seen his glory!

? Jesus is presented as a lion and as a lamb. How should each of those roles relate to your life as a disciple? How have they related in the past? What will you think about in a different way after studying this chapter? What will you *do* differently?

6

▼

Open the Seals
REVELATION 6

Now we come to the action parts of Revelation, and no chapter has more action than this one. The vivid colors and suggestion of bloody events, grabs not only our attention but especially our emotions. And that is precisely its design. The greatest motivators know that emotional stimulation provokes far more response than mere intellectual stimulation. Since God is the greatest motivator of all, it is not surprising that he seeks to arouse powerful emotions in those he is attempting to influence. As we start reading these passages, complete with their "blood and guts," work hard to visualize what John was seeing and feeling; don't read as a dispassionate scholar. Let your emotions get involved. Then you will begin to understand Revelation in the way God intended. Let your heart race with the horses!

The Four Horses (6:1-8)

6:1I watched as the Lamb opened the first of the seven seals. Then I heard one of the four living creatures say in a voice like thunder, "Come!" 2I looked, and there before me was a white horse! Its rider held a bow, and he was given a crown, and he rode out as a conqueror bent on conquest.

3When the Lamb opened the second seal, I heard the second living creature say, "Come!" 4Then another horse came out, a fiery red one. Its rider was given power to take peace from the earth and to make men slay each other. To him was given a large sword.

5When the Lamb opened the third seal, I heard the third living creature say, "Come!" I looked, and there before me was a black horse! Its rider was holding a pair of scales in his hand. 6Then I heard what sounded like a voice among the four living creatures, saying, "A quart of wheat for a day's wages, and three quarts of barley for a day's wages, and do not damage the oil and the wine!"

> *[7]When the Lamb opened the fourth seal, I heard the voice of the fourth living creature say, "Come!" [8]I looked, and there before me was a pale horse! Its rider was named Death, and Hades was following close behind him. They were given power over a fourth of the earth to kill by sword, famine and plague, and by the wild beasts of the earth.*

Picture yourself sitting in a large auditorium with a huge stage. As the curtain opens, you wonder what you are about to see. Suddenly, a voice shouts "Come!" and you hear loud hoofbeats, followed by a white horse running across the stage, its nostrils flaring and mane flowing. The rider on its back wears a crown and carries a bow of conquest. Before the shock of those sights and sounds wears off, a fiery red horse makes his entrance, ridden by a man with a large sword. Just after he rides off the stage, a third powerful horse runs across the stage in the same manner, followed by a fourth horse. The sound of the horses' hoofbeats are nearly deafening and the sights are more than captivating—they are *staggering*!

Something akin to this is what John experienced. He is left wondering what these horses symbolized, and so are we. If we were dealing with literalism rather than symbolism, we would not expect to be able to see any of the message in the scroll until all seven seals were opened. However, we are dealing with changing figures in symbolic imagery. Each seal now carries its own message. As Jesus opens each seal, a vivid image comes to us depicting some message about the tumultuous times faced by those early disciples in the midst of intense persecution. But what are the images intended to symbolize? The background of the book leads us to look for descriptions of the forces behind the persecution and to look for God's power to deal with those who brought it.

With this intent in mind, the white horse would most likely symbolize the preaching of the gospel, which was the catalyst for the persecution. The color white indicates the purity of the gospel and the crown on the rider shows the victories wrought by the preaching of the good news. A similar passage in 19:11-16 shows Jesus riding on a white horse against his enemies. Also, Zechariah 1:8-11 and 6:1-8 contain similar horse symbolism. But we must keep in mind that Revelation is merely borrowing the symbols from the prophets and applying them in the first century setting, not describing a fulfillment of them.

The bow, a weapon of war, in 6:2 further demonstrates conquest as the purpose of the rider and its horse. The key purpose of disciples in any century is conquering the world for King Jesus. (See Habakkuk 3:9 for a similar symbolic use of the bow.)

The fiery red horse (6:4) symbolizes the persecution which follows the preaching of the Word. Such persecution takes peace from the earth and causes men to slay each other. As we read this description, we are reminded of the words of Jesus in Matthew 10:34-36:

> *"Do not suppose that I have come to bring peace to the earth. I did not come to bring peace, but a sword. For I have come to turn*
> *'a man against his father,*
> *a daughter against her mother,*
> *a daughter-in-law against her mother-in-law—*
> *a man's enemies will be the members*
> *of his own household.'"*

Persecution is *inevitable* when Christians are carrying out the mission of their Master. Paul wrote in 2 Timothy 3:12: "In fact, everyone who wants to live a godly life in Christ Jesus will be persecuted." It should be obvious that living a godly life is much more than setting a good moral example. For living as a good example, we seldom receive more than minor rejection. But a godly life must include speaking out against evil and speaking up in favor of righteousness. Paul put it this way in Ephesians 5:11: "Have nothing to do with the fruitless deeds of darkness, but rather expose them." For living this kind of life, your white horse will be closely followed by those on red horses!

The black horse depicts the economic discrimination which comes in the early stages of persecution. The rider has a pair of scales in his hand, which suggests scarcity in this context (6:5-6). The color black suggests the dismal time experienced during such persecution. The scarcity of grain shows the limitation of necessities, whereas the luxuries (oil and wine) were available. Of course, the disciples had no money for these and not enough for the wheat and barley. Since all of the products mentioned were from crops, we must be dealing with discrimination rather than a time of famine brought on by failed crops. In 13:16-17, economic discrimination is clearly spelled out: "He also forced everyone, small and great, rich and poor, free and slave, to receive a mark on his right hand or on his forehead, so that no one could buy or sell unless he had the mark, which is the name of the beast or the number of his name."

The pale horse with its rider named Death were killers. The color of this horse (from *chloros*) is a pale yellowish-green, suggesting the color of a corpse. The methods of killing mentioned are commonly associated in the Bible with times of great upheaval (Ezekiel 5:14-17). Hades is mentioned in connection with death several times in Revelation (1:18, 6:8, 20:13-14). The pale horse and rider were given great power to wreak havoc. The ultimate consequences of rejecting the gospel then are felt by saint and sinner alike. The fact that this deadly duo are "given power" shows that God allows evil men the opportunity to make choices, but he is still in control and will deal with those who abuse their freedom of choice.

? Has persecution ever affected you financially in a significant way? If yes, how did you respond? If no, how do you think you would respond? Why? How do you think you would respond if persecution reached the stage described in this chapter?

Souls Under the Altar (6:9-11)

[9]When he opened the fifth seal, I saw under the altar the souls of those who had been slain because of the word of God and the testimony they had maintained. [10]They called out in a loud voice, "How long, Sovereign Lord, holy and true, until you judge the inhabitants of the earth and avenge our blood?" [11]Then each of them was given a white robe, and they were told to wait a little longer, until the number of their fellow servants and brothers who were to be killed as they had been was completed.

The fifth seal introduces the martyred saints who died in the persecution. The first four seals showed how the persecution developed and now this seal shows the tragic end for those engulfed in it. The slain ones were "under the altar."

Since blood was poured at the base of the altar in OT sacrifices (Leviticus 4:7), we have here the idea that the martyrs are a sacrifice to God. The martyrs wanted to know how long the persecutors were going to be able to continue in their horrible quest on the earth. Persecution began to intensify first in Jerusalem, then Nero widened its scope into Rome, and in John's day, Domitian was spreading it through much of the empire.

When the slain were asking God to avenge their blood (6:10), they were requesting that God vindicate his righteous Cause much more than they were asking for individual revenge. Light and darkness were locked in deadly conflict, and those who had sacrificed their lives for the light did not want their deaths to be in vain. Unavenged blood cries out from the ground for justice! (Genesis 4:10). And God's servants often cry out for this kind of justice to prevail, as the book of Psalms attests. (Scan through Psalms with this concept in mind.)

An interesting concept is introduced in 6:11 that is reinforced by a number of other Biblical passages. God has a limit on the amount of sin he will allow before bringing retribution. When that limit is reached, nothing will stop his judgment from falling on those to whom it is due. Back in Genesis 15:16, God said that he was timing the Israelites' conquest of Canaan to coincide with the sins of the Amorites reaching their limit. Jesus said something similar in Matthew 23:32-36 about the Jews of his day. From man's time-bound perspective, much injustice and unfairness seems to reign unchecked, but from God's eternal perspective, nothing will escape its just rewards!

Great Earthquake Judgment (6:12-17)

> [12]I watched as he opened the sixth seal. There was a great earthquake. The sun turned black like sackcloth made of goat hair, the whole moon turned blood red, [13]and the stars in the sky fell to earth, as late figs drop from a fig tree when shaken by a strong wind. [14]The sky receded like a scroll, rolling up, and every mountain and island was removed from its place.
>
> [15]Then the kings of the earth, the princes, the generals, the rich, the mighty, and every slave and every free man hid in caves and among the rocks of the mountains. [16]They called to the mountains and the rocks, "Fall on us and hide us from the face of him who sits on the throne and from the wrath of the Lamb! [17]For the great day of their wrath has come, and who can stand?"

The contents of the sixth seal show God's judgment in response to the prayers of those seen in the vision of the fifth seal (6:10). This judgment comes in the form of an earthquake, a feared natural calamity that was all too familiar to the residents of Asia Minor. We are much too early in Revelation for the final Day of Judgment to be introduced. Instead, God is promising to deal powerfully with the persecutors as he metes out justice to them. The symbolism in the Old Testament often pictured temporal judgment against nations with the same type of graphic language. To see examples of such usage, read the following passages with similar images.

Earthquake

> "'*In my zeal and fiery wrath I declare that at that time there shall be a great earthquake in the land of Israel. [20]The fish of the sea, the birds of the air, the beasts of the field, every creature that moves along the ground, and all the people on the face of the earth will tremble at my presence. The mountains will be overturned, the cliffs will crumble and every wall will fall to the ground. [21]I will summon a sword against Gog on all my mountains, declares the Sovereign LORD. Every man's sword will be against his brother. [22]I will execute judgment upon him with plague and bloodshed; I will pour down torrents of rain, hailstones and burning sulfur on him and on his troops and on the many nations with him. [23]And so I will show my greatness and my holiness, and I will make myself known in the sight of many nations. Then they will know that I am the Lord.'*"*
> *(Ezekiel 38:19-23)*

> *Before them the earth shakes,*
>   *the sky trembles,*
> *the sun and moon are darkened,*
>   *and the stars no longer shine. (Joel 2:10)*

> *"This is what the LORD Almighty says: 'In a little while I will once more shake the heavens and the earth, the sea and the dry land. [7]I will shake all nations, and the desired of all nations will come, and I will fill this house with glory,' says the LORD Almighty." (Haggai 2:6-7)*

Sun and Moon

> *"I clothe the sky with darkness*
>   *and make sackcloth its covering." (Isaiah 50:3)*

"The sun will be turned to darkness
and the moon to blood
before the coming of the great and dreadful day of the LORD."
(Joel 2:31)

Stars Falling

All the stars of the heavens will be dissolved
and the sky rolled up like a scroll;
all the starry host will fall
like withered leaves from the vine,
like shriveled figs from the fig tree. (Isaiah 34:4)

Hills and Islands Moved

I looked at the mountains,
and they were quaking;
all the hills were swaying. (Jeremiah 4:24)

The mountains quake before him
and the hills melt away.
The earth trembles at his presence,
the world and all who live in it. (Nahum 1:5)

Mountains and Rocks

The high places of wickedness will be destroyed—
it is the sin of Israel.
Thorns and thistles will grow up
and cover their altars.
Then they will say to the mountains, "Cover us!"
and to the hills, "Fall on us!." (Hosea 10:8)

Take the time to read each of these passages in their context. You will discover that they are applied to different nations as God's time of punishment approached. Clearly the
figures are symbols and not intended to be literal. In the case
of Haggai 2 (quoted above), the author of Hebrews declared
that the impending destruction of Jerusalem was a fulfillment
of Haggai's prophecy (Hebrews 12:26-29). This judgment
would mark the end of Biblical Judaism (for the sacrifices
would never again be offered) and the exaltation of the church
as the kingdom of God on earth. The point is that all such
symbols in the prophets depicted the downfall of *nations* rather

than the end of the world. Those unfamiliar with prophetic language often mistakenly assume that such graphic language must be describing the "end times," but once we begin to read this language in its original context, the matter comes into clearer focus.

Revelation 6, with its six seals, follows a very logical progression. First, the preaching of the gospel; second, the persecution which it prompts in ungodly hearts; third, economic discrimination as the milder form of the persecution; fourth, the devastating consequences of the world's rejection of truth on saved and unsaved alike (for different reasons, of course); fifth, the cries of the martyred disciples for God's righteous vengeance to be satisfied; and sixth, the announcement by God of impending judgment in response to those cries. The bigger picture of persecution's causes, effects, and ultimate punishment is now better understood. With that, chapter 6 concludes.

? Now that we are dealing more with the symbolic language in Revelation, what seems clear to you about it and what seems puzzling? The souls under the altar were impatient about God dealing justice to the wicked. What circumstances in your life make you impatient with God? Do you often question if he (or others) are treating you fairly? What is the danger of focusing too much on "fairness"?

7

▼

Hold the Show
REVELATION 7

Revelation 7 forms an interlude between the sixth and seventh seals, answering the question of how God's children would be affected by God's judgments against the wicked, as described in the sixth seal. Would they be subject to the same destructive forces as the ones whom God was punishing? In the first part of the chapter, we find that 144,000 servants are sealed for protection, and in the remainder, a great multitude are praising God. The same group is viewed from two different vantage points. On earth, the persecuted saints will be numbered and protected by God, and in heaven they will be delivered into the wonderful presence of their Father. Thus, they are pictured first as the redeemed *militant* (as God's spiritual army) and then as the redeemed *triumphant* (as God's eternally saved family).

144,000 of God's Servants Sealed (7:1-8)

7:1After this I saw four angels standing at the four corners of the earth, holding back the four winds of the earth to prevent any wind from blowing on the land or on the sea or on any tree. 2Then I saw another angel coming up from the east, having the seal of the living God. He called out in a loud voice to the four angels who had been given power to harm the land and the sea: 3"Do not harm the land or the sea or the trees until we put a seal on the foreheads of the servants of our God." 4Then I heard the number of those who were sealed: 144,000 from all the tribes of Israel.

5From the tribe of Judah 12,000 were sealed,
  from the tribe of Reuben 12,000,
  from the tribe of Gad 12,000,
  6from the tribe of Asher 12,000,
  from the tribe of Naphtali 12,000,
  from the tribe of Manasseh 12,000,

[7]from the tribe of Simeon 12,000,
from the tribe of Levi 12,000,
from the tribe of Issachar 12,000,
[8]from the tribe of Zebulun 12,000,
from the tribe of Joseph 12,000,
from the tribe of Benjamin 12,000.

The angels at the four corners of the earth are holding back the judgments of God until God's servants can be protected from the onslaught. (See Jeremiah 49:36 and Daniel 7:2-5 for the destroying wind figure.) The mention of four corners of the earth does not suggest that the writer believed the earth to be flat. It was a way of designating the entire earth. Isaiah 11:12 speaks of the "four quarters of the earth" and Jeremiah 49:36 speaks of the "four quarters of the heavens."

From the direction of the sun's rising comes an angel with the seal of God. Historically, when something was "sealed," it had received the stamp of ownership. For example, God's normal seal for Christians is the Holy Spirit (Ephesians 1:13, 4:30). Satan's servants were likewise sealed ("marked") by him (Revelation 13:16-17, 14:9, 16:2, etc.).

In Revelation 7, we find that ownership guarantees protection. The angel was to seal the servants of God on their foreheads, which indicates that they were eligible for protection because their *minds* were devoted to the service of their Maker. The sealing thus identified them in order to protect them from the judgments of God which were fast approaching. The idea of sealing for protection during a time of God's judgment traces back to a similar usage in Ezekiel 9:1-6, a passage that should be read carefully.

> *Then I heard him call out in a loud voice, "Bring the guards of the city here, each with a weapon in his hand." And I saw six men coming from the direction of the upper gate, which faces north, each with a deadly weapon in his hand. With them was a man clothed in linen who had a writing kit at his side. They came in and stood beside the bronze altar.*
>
> *Now the glory of the God of Israel went up from above the cherubim, where it had been, and moved to the threshold of the temple. Then the LORD called to the man clothed in linen who had the writing kit at his side and said to him, "Go throughout the city of Jerusalem and put a mark on the*

*foreheads of those who grieve and lament over all the detest-
able things that are done in it."*
    *As I listened, he said to the others, "Follow him through the
city and kill, without showing pity or compassion. Slaughter
old men, young men and maidens, women and children, but do
not touch anyone who has the mark. Begin at my sanctuary."
So they began with the elders who were in front of the temple.*

The number of servants sealed was 144,000—12,000 from
each of the twelve tribes. Obviously a key issue here is the
identity of the 144,000. Who were they? Since the persecutors were often Jews, or were aided by Jews, it should be
obvious that the twelve tribes mentioned in our present text
were not literally the twelve tribes of the Jews. In fact, they
were guilty of bringing about God's judgment due to their
persecution of Christians! Therefore, we must of necessity
be dealing with a spiritualized usage of the twelve tribes.
(The 144,000 are mentioned again in Revelation 14 and will
be discussed in that context in Chapter 11.)
    Let's begin by considering the numbers mentioned. We
know that twelve is the symbol for God's group or organization. There were twelve tribes in the OT Jewish nation and
twelve apostles in the NT church leadership. At the outset, it is
safe to assume that those protected could be none other than
the disciples undergoing the persecution. Revelation was written to address their problems and bring them encouragement.
Therefore, the 144,000 must symbolically describe them. We
know that Christians are now the true Jews (Romans 2:28-29,
Philippians 3:3). We also know that the church is now the true
Israel of God, as Galatians 6:15-16 makes plain: "Neither circumcision nor uncircumcision means anything; what counts
is a new creation. Peace and mercy to all who follow this rule,
even to the Israel of God."
    The names of the twelve tribes in 7:5-8 provide us with a
further indication that a spiritualized usage is intended. They
are not the same as the twelve mentioned in the OT setting
when they received their inheritance (Joshua 13-19). Judah is
mentioned first because it was the tribe out of which Jesus came.
(See Genesis 49:10 for a Messianic prophecy about a ruler from
this tribe.) Levi is included in the list, although the Levites were
not included in the inheritance of land territories and were

omitted from some OT lists as a result. (See Numbers 1 and 2.) Since all Christians are priests (1 Peter 2:5-9), John must be writing about spiritual Israel in our present passage. Dan and Ephraim were excluded from the list, no doubt because the cities of Dan and Bethel (in the territory of Ephraim) were centers of calf worship under Jereboam. Also, Joseph's name was included here rather than the names of his two sons (Ephraim and Manasseh) who both inherited land allotments. To the Bible reader, the name of Joseph has only good connotations.

Each of the twelve tribes in 7:5-8 is numbered at 12,000. The number of God's group is multiplied by the number of ultimate completeness (1,000) in the case of each tribe. The lesson is that all people in God's kingdom are going to receive his blessings of protection. None would be overlooked; all would be protected. However, another question arises. To what *extent* would they be protected, since they were already dying for their faith? The only logical conclusion is that they would be protected spiritually but not physically. And isn't this true for all Christians in all ages? We undergo many of the same trials in life—severe and ordinary—as do non-Christians, but with a different perspective. As Jesus put it in Matthew 10:28, "Do not be afraid of those who kill the body but cannot kill the soul. Rather, be afraid of the One who can destroy both soul and body in hell." 1 Corinthians 10:13 gives us this promise:

> *No temptation has seized you except what is common to man. And God is faithful; he will not let you be tempted beyond what you can bear. But when you are tempted, he will also provide a way out so that you can stand up under it.*

Note that disciples are not promised the *removal* of the temptation, but the help to *endure* it.

A similar lesson is taught in 11:1-2. In that passage, the temple of God is measured and counted, but the outer court is not measured. It was to be given over to "the Gentiles" (non-Christians) to trample on it. Thus, the spiritual life—but not the physical life—was measured for protection. While God promises to work *in all things* for the good of his people (Romans 8:28), Christians are not guaranteed that no physical harm will occur to them. We may suffer from accident or disease, and we will all die. Some of us will live to old age and others will die young. But if we are the children of God, he will never abandon us in physical tests (1 Peter 1: 5-6) and we must not allow such challenges to move us away from our commitment to Jesus as Lord. By the power of God, we can endure to the end of our lives, even if that end should come at the hand of persecutors. We must never back down, never give up and never wimp out! The challenge to the readers of Revelation is *death before denial!* In all situations, God knows what we are facing and will give us the power to face it triumphantly.

? Were you surprised that more protection of a physical nature was not promised in Revelation? How do you feel about the physical calamities and challenges faced by disciples—do you think God should intervene more? Explain your answer. How should we view physical and emotional challenges when they come into our lives or the lives of our families? What will help you to do that? (See 2 Peter 2:9.)

An Innumerable Multitude in Heaven (7:9-17)

9After this I looked and there before me was a great multitude that no one could count, from every nation, tribe, people and language, standing before the throne and in front of the Lamb. They were wearing white robes and were holding palm branches in their hands. 10And they cried out in a loud voice:

"Salvation belongs to our God,
who sits on the throne,
and to the Lamb."

11All the angels were standing around the throne and around the elders and the four living creatures. They fell down on their faces before the throne and worshiped God, 12saying:

"Amen!
Praise and glory
and wisdom and thanks and honor
and power and strength
be to our God for ever and ever.
Amen!"

13Then one of the elders asked me, "These in white robes— who are they, and where did they come from?"
14I answered, "Sir, you know."

> *And he said, "These are they who have come out of the*
> *great tribulation; they have washed their robes and made them*
> *white in the blood of the Lamb. [15]Therefore,*
> *"they are before the throne of God*
> *and serve him day and night in his temple;*
> *and he who sits on the throne will spread his tent over them.*
> *[16]Never again will they hunger; never again will they thirst.*
> *The sun will not beat upon them, nor any scorching heat.*
> *[17]For the Lamb at the center of the throne will be their shep-*
> *herd;*
> *he will lead them to springs of living water.*
> *And God will wipe away every tear from their eyes."*

The next vision takes us far from the earth with its perse-
cutions and calamities. Now we see in heaven a great multitude which seemed to be innumerable (7:9). On earth, the
saints had to be counted for protection. In heaven they have
been delivered from the circumstances requiring protection,
and therefore, they no longer need to be numbered! Amen!
This vast throng was comprised of people of all nations and
backgrounds. This shows what the nature of the church on
earth is to be—a large family, diverse in numerous ways, but
having the same heart for Jesus and his mission.

The white robes symbolize both victory and purity
(7:9, 7:14).

The palm branches (7:9) were associated with festivities at
the Feast of Tabernacles when the fall harvest had been gathered (Leviticus 23:34-43). When Jesus entered Jerusalem in
what we often call the "triumphant entry," the people spread
palm branches for his path (John 12:13, Matthew 21:8).

In the midst of persecution, the disciples were crying out
for vengeance (6:10), but now in heaven they were crying out
loudly about how great God was and how great it was to be in
his presence (7:10). Whatever heaven is actually going to be
like, we are going to absolutely be thrilled with it forever and
ever! The specific identity of the ones in white robes is given
in 7:14. They were cleansed by the blood of Christ, which
occurs when we are baptized into him and his death (Romans
6:3-4, Acts 22:16) The verb translated as "have come" shows a
continual process. As the saints were dying during the time of
persecution, they were being ushered into the presence of God
and the Lamb.

The description of this victorious setting in 7:15-17 is reminiscent of Revelation 21:1-4. Victory is secure. Those who have been delivered now have the perfect Presence (God), the perfect protection and the perfect provisions. The promise of the Psalmist has been fulfilled abundantly for these overcomers— "Those who sow in tears will reap with songs of joy" (Psalm 126:5). Let us join those before God's throne and exclaim with them, "Amen and Amen!"

? How real is heaven to you? Do you see heaven more as a "consolation prize" when life on earth ends, or do you eagerly anticipate going there? Examine your heart on this issue and explain your answer. What do you need to change about your view, and how are you going to do it?

8
▼

Blow the Trumpets
REVELATION 8 AND 9

Now that the 144,000 servants of God have been sealed for protection, the Lamb can open the seventh seal. When it is opened, it leads to another series of seven—seven trumpets. As in the case of the seals, an interlude will occur between the sixth and seventh trumpets. In Revelation 15-16 we will be introduced to another series of seven, the bowls of wrath. At that point, we will see a very close relationship to the trumpets. But now, let's read John's introduction to the sounding of the trumpets.

The Trumpets Introduced (8:1-6)

> *8:1When he opened the seventh seal, there was silence in heaven for about half an hour.*
> *2And I saw the seven angels who stand before God, and to them were given seven trumpets.*
> *3Another angel, who had a golden censer, came and stood at the altar. He was given much incense to offer, with the prayers of all the saints, on the golden altar before the throne. 4The smoke of the incense, together with the prayers of the saints, went up before God from the angel's hand. 5Then the angel took the censer, filled it with fire from the altar, and hurled it on the earth; and there came peals of thunder, rumblings, flashes of lightning and an earthquake.*
> *6Then the seven angels who had the seven trumpets prepared to sound them.*

The half-hour silence (8:1) may stand for God's delayed judgments against the enemies of the church. Certainly the ones under the altar in 6:10 thought he was taking too long! God is never anxious to mete out judgment. As Ezekiel 33:11 states: "Say to them, 'As surely as I live, declares the Sovereign LORD, I take no pleasure in the death of the wicked, but rather that they turn from their ways and live.'" Perhaps more to the point is 2 Peter 3:9, as it describes why the end of the world has not yet occurred: "The Lord is not slow in keeping his promise, as some understand slowness. He is patient with you, not wanting anyone to perish, but everyone to come to repentance."

The silence surely must denote the impending wrath of God against the wicked. In the vision, it created a dramatic effect like the calm before the storm. Habakkuk used these words in a similar manner: "But the LORD is in his holy temple; let all the earth be silent before him" (Habakkuk 2:20). An old hymn uses these words to call for a reverent attitude in a public worship setting, but that is not the emphasis of the prophet. It's as if he were saying, "Brace yourself, for the hand of God is about to fall, and nothing can stop it!" As we examine the symbolism of the trumpets, we will see that they are a warning to the world. Therefore, both ideas—delayed judgment and impending wrath—are likely intended by the silence.

The altar at which the angel stood suggests the idea of the altar of incense before the veil of the tabernacle. The incense represents petitions made to God for justice against the enemies. Back in 5:8, the incense was said to be the prayers of the saints, and in 8:4 the incense is combined with the prayers of the saints. The intercession of Christ and the Holy Spirit in our behalf may be intended here (Romans 8:26, 34; Hebrews 7:25; 1 John 2:1). The result of all of this intercession was the action of the angel in 8:5. Fire was hurled to the earth, showing God's displeasure with the current state of affairs and his intention to do something about it.

After the fire was thrown to the earth (8:5) announcing that God was going to act, the seven angels lined up ready to blow their trumpets. Trumpets were used for warnings in the Old Testament (Ezekiel 33:3-6, Joel 2:1). The sounding of the trumpets in Revelation signifies a call to repentance on the part of the persecutors. God always warns before executing judgments, as Amos 3:7 states: "Surely the Sovereign LORD does nothing without revealing his plan to his servants the prophets."

? Prayer which is both persistent and urgent gains the attention of God. When our
prayers are not being answered in the way we think they should, we need to examine ourselves and our prayer life. Are we righteous? (James 5:16). Are we praying with right motives? (James 4:2-3). Are we persistent? (Luke 18:1-8). Are we full of

faith? (Mark 11:22-24). Are we urgent? Read the account of Jacob's all-night wrestling match with the angel of God (Genesis 32:24-30). Quiet times with God are good; *loud* times are often better!

The First Four Trumpets: Nature Affected (8:7-13)

> *⁷The first angel sounded his trumpet, and there came hail and fire mixed with blood, and it was hurled down upon the earth. A third of the earth was burned up, a third of the trees were burned up, and all the green grass was burned up.*
>
> *⁸The second angel sounded his trumpet, and something like a huge mountain, all ablaze, was thrown into the sea. A third of the sea turned into blood, ⁹a third of the living creatures in the sea died, and a third of the ships were destroyed.*
>
> *¹⁰The third angel sounded his trumpet, and a great star, blazing like a torch, fell from the sky on a third of the rivers and on the springs of water—¹¹the name of the star is Wormwood. A third of the waters turned bitter, and many people died from the waters that had become bitter.*
>
> *¹²The fourth angel sounded his trumpet, and a third of the sun was struck, a third of the moon, and a third of the stars, so that a third of them turned dark. A third of the day was without light, and also a third of the night.*
>
> *¹³As I watched, I heard an eagle that was flying in midair call out in a loud voice: "Woe! Woe! Woe to the inhabitants of the earth, because of the trumpet blasts about to be sounded by the other three angels!"*

Just as the first four seals are closely related in symbolic meaning, the first four trumpets are as well. Different aspects of nature will be affected: first the land, then the sea, followed by the inland waters and finally the heavenly bodies. In each case, a third of the target is destroyed. The effect is significant but not totally destructive, for we are dealing with warnings at this point. How are we to interpret this first series of trumpets? They are certainly a blow against the evil world, as promised by God in the sixth seal: his servants would not go unheard nor would sinners go unpunished. However, whether the symbols simply denote a general type of punishment or something more specific is not clear. If something specific was intended, natural calamity is as good a conjecture as any. Asia Minor was all too familiar with earthquakes, volcanoes and other forms of natural disasters. God does use such calamities to induce repentance and such may well have been in view here.

The first trumpet leads to hail and fire mixed with blood being cast down on the earth (8:7). The figures of hail and fire were used in Isaiah 30:30 to show God's judgment against Assyria. "The LORD will cause men to hear his majestic voice and will make them see his arm coming down with raging anger and consuming fire, with cloudburst, thunderstorm and hail." The wording reminds us of the plagues in Egypt as well (Exodus 9:24). The mention of blood hurled down could suggest the return of blood upon the heads of the wicked. Such reaping of the consequences of one's own sins is Biblically depicted in numerous places (Leviticus 20:9-27, Joshua 2:19, 2 Samuel 1:16, etc.). Paul used the figure in Acts 18:6 with these words:

> But when the Jews opposed Paul and became abusive, he shook out his clothes in protest and said to them, "Your blood be on your own heads! I am clear of my responsibility. From now on I will go to the Gentiles."

The second trumpet introduces a vision of a great burning mountain being cast into the sea (8:8-9). Mountains often signified nations in the Old Testament, and their being cast down shows their fall from power. In Isaiah 2:2 God promised to establish his mountain (kingdom) which was to be exalted above all other mountains (kingdoms). Similarly, speaking against the nation of Babylon, Jeremiah said:

> "I am against you, O destroying mountain,
> you who destroy the whole earth,'
> declares the LORD.
> 'I will stretch out my hand against you,
> roll you off the cliffs,
> and make you a burned-out mountain." (Jeremiah 51:25)

The effects of this trumpet seem more severe than the first one, in that the amount of blood in the vision increases. A third of the sea was turned into blood. In a literal example, the first Egyptian plague caused all of the rivers and lakes to be turned into blood (Exodus 7:14-24).

Trumpet three sounds, leading to a great blazing star falling on a third of the fresh waters on earth (8:10-11). When John was seeing these dramatic visions, he must have been overwhelmed visually and emotionally. He would have not been intellectually trying to do what we are doing in cross-referencing the various symbols used. Probably he gave much thought to these things later, but not at the expense of losing the main lesson intended—the awesome power of God would be unleashed against the enemies of his people! It is natural to delve into the figures used in order to discover what we can about their Biblical background. But we must not lose the dramatic effect by looking too closely at the trees. Be amazed at the forest!

Stars (8:10), like mountains, were used to describe nations or perhaps heads of nations. The king of Babylon was promised defeat in these words:

> *How you have fallen from heaven,*
> *O morning star, son of the dawn!*
> *You have been cast down to the earth,*
> *you who once laid low the nations!" (Isaiah 14:12)*

Wormwood (8:11) was a bitter type of wood mentioned several times in the Old Testament in connection with sinning against God. (You will have to use another translation besides the NIV, which normally translates it as "bitter food.") A good reference similar to our present passage is Jeremiah 9:15: "therefore thus says the Lord of hosts, the God of Israel, 'behold, I will feed them, this people, with wormwood and give them poisoned water to drink'" (NASV[1]). The point is that sinning against the Lord and his people will have dire consequences in time as well as in eternity.

Trumpet four ushered in an impact on the sun, moon and stars (8:12). These figures were often used in the Old Testament to show calamity against political powers. A good example is found in Isaiah 13:9-10, which is a warning against the nation of Babylon.

> *See, the day of the LORD is coming*
> *—a cruel day, with wrath and fierce anger—*
> *to make the land desolate*
> *and destroy the sinners within it.*

The stars of heaven and their constellations
   will not show their light.
The rising sun will be darkened
   and the moon will not give its light.

Other similar passages using apocalyptic language to describe the punishment of nations are Isaiah 19:1, 34:2-8; Ezekiel 32:1-10; Joel 2:1-11, 28-32; Amos 8:9; Zephaniah 1:14-2:3.

The darkness in 8:12 is reminiscent of the ninth Egyptian plague (Exodus 10:21-29).

This section ends with an eagle flying in midair announcing that three woes are about to come (8:13). The identification of the remaining trumpets as "woes" shows that their effects are worse than the first four. The phrase "the inhabitants of the earth" is found seven times in Revelation, all indicating the pagan world (6:10, 8:13, 11:10, 13:8, 13:14, 17:2 and 17:8). For their sins against God and his saints, they will face the mighty hand of their Maker.

The Fifth Trumpet: Internal Decay (9:1-12)

9:1The fifth angel sounded his trumpet, and I saw a star that had fallen from the sky to the earth. The star was given the key to the shaft of the Abyss. 2When he opened the Abyss, smoke rose from it like the smoke from a gigantic furnace. The sun and sky were darkened by the smoke from the Abyss. 3And out of the smoke locusts came down upon the earth and were given power like that of scorpions of the earth. 4They were told not to harm the grass of the earth or any plant or tree, but only those people who did not have the seal of God on their foreheads. 5They were not given power to kill them, but only to torture them for five months. And the agony they suffered was like that of the sting of a scorpion when it strikes a man. 6During those days men will seek death, but will not find it; they will long to die, but death will elude them.

7The locusts looked like horses prepared for battle. On their heads they wore something like crowns of gold, and their faces resembled human faces. 8Their hair was like women's hair, and their teeth were like lions' teeth. 9They had breastplates like breastplates of iron, and the sound of their wings was like the thundering of many horses and chariots rushing into battle. 10They had tails and stings like scorpions, and in their tails they had power to torment people for five months. 11They had

as king over them the angel of the Abyss, whose name in He-
brew is Abaddon, and in Greek, Apollyon.
    [12]The first woe is past; two other woes are yet to come.

The first woe, or fifth trumpet, introduces the reader to an
unusual locust plague. The star with the key to the abyss (the
residence of demons—Luke 8:31) appears to be none other
than Satan (9:1-2). Of him, Jesus said, "I saw Satan fall like
lightning from heaven" (Luke 10:18). He has been given authority by God to lead the demonic world. In 9:11, he is called
"Abaddon" or "Apollyon," which means "Destroyer." Opening the abyss allowed smoke to pour out, blocking the light
of the sun. Satan's lies always block the light of truth, which
seems to be the point here.

As the smoke escaped, it then took on the form of locusts
(9:3). Locust hordes were always dreaded because of their destructive power on nature and agriculture. The eighth plague
in Egypt was a locust plague (Exodus 10:1-20). Joel describes
a locust plague with similar language in chapter two of his
prophecy (2:1-11). In Revelation 9, the locusts had the power
of scorpions to inflict pain. Locusts and scorpions are used
symbolically to describe the forces of evil. Jesus promised his
apostles power over these forces with these words: "I have
given you authority to trample on snakes and scorpions and
to overcome all the power of the enemy; nothing will harm
you" (Luke 10:19).

The most likely interpretation of this fifth trumpet or first
woe is that internal decay is being portrayed. Rome was decaying from the inside out as her excesses and lack of restraint
took their toll. Satan does his job well—at times too well, for
even the wicked began to see the fallacy of the path they are
traveling. The wages of sin are high indeed. What begins looking wonderful ends with devastation. Satan's plan is not unlike our nearly unbridled credit system with its "buy now, pay
later" mentality. Satan tries to lure us into sinning now, knowing we will pay later with tremendously high interest. God
always advises us to pay up front by obeying his principles,
knowing that later we will reap tremendous dividends.

Sin feeds on itself. The progression found in Romans
1:18-32 is irreversible in any society not following God. And
at some point, even those caught up in the web of sin can see

pain. Over the years, a life
cynicism. As Fontaine sang
ie dream I dreamed." Con-
ses:

> *"Why is light given to those in misery,*
> *and life to the bitter of soul,*
> *to those who long for death that does not come,*
> *who search for it more than for hidden treasure,*
> *who are filled with gladness*
> *and rejoice when they reach the grave?" (Job 3:20-22)*

> *And I declared that the dead,*
> *who had already died,*
> *are happier than the living,*
> *who are still alive.*
> *But better than both*
> *is he who has not yet been,*
> *who has not seen the evil*
> *that is done under the sun. (Ecclesiastes 4:2-3)*

> *"'Wherever I banish them, all the survivors of this evil na-*
> *tion will prefer death to life, declares the LORD Almighty.'"*
> *(Jeremiah 8:3)*

When the Bible speaks of God punishing those who choose
a life of sin, it is important to realize something about how
God delivers that punishment. More often than not, the punishment is nothing more than the consequences of sin in the
life of the person choosing to sin. I do not picture God saying,
"Okay, I've just about had it with him, and now I am going to
really get him!" God hates sin, true enough, but he also hates
to see people hurting, even for their own sins. He said in Ezekiel
18:23: "Do I take any pleasure in the death of the wicked?
declares the Sovereign LORD. Rather, am I not pleased when
they turn from their ways and live?" Sin carries its own seeds
of self-destruction, and since God has provided us with the
power of choice, our exercise of the wrong choices may be
viewed as God's punishment. More correctly, we should picture God being on our side wanting desperately for us to choose
righteousness and be blessed greatly.

The Sixth Trumpet: External Invasion (9:13-21)

> [13]*The sixth angel sounded his trumpet, and I heard a voice coming from the horns of the golden altar that is before God.* [14]*It said to the sixth angel who had the trumpet, "Release the four angels who are bound at the great river Euphrates." [15]And the four angels who had been kept ready for this very hour and day and month and year were released to kill a third of mankind. [16]The number of the mounted troops was two hundred million. I heard their number.*
>
> [17]*The horses and riders I saw in my vision looked like this: Their breastplates were fiery red, dark blue, and yellow as sulfur. The heads of the horses resembled the heads of lions, and out of their mouths came fire, smoke and sulfur. [18]A third of mankind was killed by the three plagues of fire, smoke and sulfur that came out of their mouths. [19]The power of the horses was in their mouths and in their tails; for their tails were like snakes, having heads with which they inflict injury.*
>
> [20]*The rest of mankind that were not killed by these plagues still did not repent of the work of their hands; they did not stop worshipping demons, and idols of gold, silver, bronze, stone and wood—idols that cannot see or hear or walk. [21]Nor did they repent of their murders, their magic arts, their sexual immorality or their thefts.*

The sixth trumpet (second woe) is introduced with a command to release four angels who had been kept from bringing a severe judgment against mankind (9:15). They were held back by God until sins had reached the limit he would allow and the time was ripe ("this very hour and day and month and year"). God is in control, in spite of what we may think. He knows the day when a nation will rise to power and the day when it will fall. And he knows the birthday and death day of every person. "All the days ordained for me were written in your book before one of them came to be" (Psalm 139:16). When we are tempted to think the wicked are getting away with too much and that life is unfair, we had better trust God and his timing. At the Judgment Day, all such thinking will be shown to be humanistic folly. No one ultimately gets away with anything.

The agents used by the angels were horsemen, two hundred million strong! The horses and riders are described in fear-inducing detail. Their breastplates were vividly bright and the horses worse than dragons, with fire coming out of their mouths and tails like venomous snakes! What does all of this mean? Simply that God had millions of powerful agents lined up to inflict evil against those who opposed him and his servants. A good case can be made that the trumpets represented the three key areas that weakened the Roman empire: natural calamities (trumpets 1-4), internal decay (trumpet 5) and external invasion (trumpet 6). The borders of Rome were always subject to invasion by some fierce warriors such as the Parthians.

God was showing John in no uncertain terms who had the real power, and it wasn't Caesar! Back in Elisha's day, God made another such demonstration. The servant of the prophet arose one morning to see the entire city surrounded by enemy armies. Like many of us, he panicked. Then came the demonstration.

> *When the servant of the man of God got up and went out early the next morning, an army with horses and chariots had surrounded the city. "Oh, my lord, what shall we do?" the servant asked.*
>
> *"Don't be afraid," the prophet answered. "Those who are with us are more than those who are with them."*
>
> *And Elisha prayed, "O LORD, open his eyes so he may see." Then the LORD opened the servant's eyes, and he looked and saw the hills full of horses and chariots of fire all around Elisha. (2 Kings 6:15-17)*

God has his innumerable hosts of angels to serve him and to serve us (Hebrews 1:14). He sent one angel into the camp of the Assyrians during the time of King Hezekiah and he killed 185,000 men during the night. Just imagine what the more than twelve legions could have done if Jesus had requested their services! (Matthew 26:53). If one legion was comprised of 6,000 or more, then Jesus could have immediately had more than 72,000 angels at his disposal. And if we were trying to be foolishly literal, then these angels would not have had any problem destroying thirteen billion in a night! ($72,000 \times 185,000 = 13,320,000,000$.) Of course such literalism really is senseless. God in these visions is dramatizing his power in order to get men to quit doubting and fretting. He wants us to have faith and loosen up! Everything is really going to turn out just fine, if we hold on to our faith in an all-knowing, all-powerful God.

In the final two verses of Revelation 9, we learn that the trumpet calls of warning did not have a significant impact on those to whom they were sent. Even in the midst of calamity, evil men hold on to the sins that are destroying them. God deeply desires for all of his enemies to repent and not be destroyed. He is kind (Romans 2:4) in order to induce repentance. If that does not work, then discipline is sure to follow. And if that fails, he will crush those entrenched in sin. He may be rejected and abused, but he will not be mocked. His judgment train may take a long time to roll into the station, but when it does, it will not be derailed!

Even though the trumpets were warning calls to the rebellious, the letters to the churches demonstrated clearly that God is always seeking to produce total repentance in his own people. If we are not being moved to repent on a continual basis, we had better read these passages in Revelation again. It is far better to be among the righteous in the hands of a loving God than to be among sinners in the hands of an angry God! Let his love and his righteous judgment move you to take serving him very, very seriously. Truly, he is sifting out the hearts of men before his judgment seat.

? Which type of circumstances in your life move you to repentance most quickly— blessings or discipline? (Read Romans 2:4 after you answer.) What does your answer to the question reveal about your heart? How can you grow in the area of deeply desiring repentance and radical change? Are you too satisfied with your present spiritual condition or maturity level? Explain.

9

▼

An End, but Not *the* End
REVELATION 10 AND 11

When is the end not really the end? Read on and you will find out. Just as an interlude came between the sixth and seventh seals, another comes between the sixth and seventh trumpets. Both interludes answered questions—the first being the question of how the people of God would be affected by the judgments God brought on the world. This second one answers John's question (whether he asked it or not) about the length of the message he was to receive. Since the last trumpet normally signified the end of the world (1 Corinthians 15:52), John might naturally have assumed that when this trumpet sounded in his visions, the climax would have been reached and the revelation ended. However, the visions in Revelation 10 showed him that such was not the case. A longer message was to come even after the final trumpet was blown. In fact, half the book was yet to be revealed.

Sweet and Sour (10:1-11)

10:1Then I saw another mighty angel coming down from heaven. He was robed in a cloud, with a rainbow above his head; his face was like the sun, and his legs were like fiery pillars. 2He was holding a little scroll, which lay open in his hand. He planted his right foot on the sea and his left foot on the land, 3and he gave a loud shout like the roar of a lion. When he shouted, the voices of the seven thunders spoke. 4And when the seven thunders spoke, I was about to write; but I heard a voice from heaven say, "Seal up what the seven thunders have said and do not write it down."

5Then the angel I had seen standing on the sea and on the land raised his right hand to heaven. 6And he swore by him who lives for ever and ever, who created the heavens and all that is in them, the earth and all that is in it, and the sea and all that is in it, and said, "There will be no more delay! 7But in

the days when the seventh angel is about to sound his trumpet,
the mystery of God will be accomplished, just as he announced
to his servants the prophets."

The angel introducing this vision is awesome in appearance, similar to that of Jesus in Revelation 1. He is holding a little scroll, which John later will eat (10:10). The planting of one foot on sea and one on earth may show the universality of the message he brought. His shout as a lion roaring (10:3) suggests a not-so-happy announcement. (See Joel 3:16 and Amos 3:8 for other uses of the figure.) The seven thunders indicate a premonition of divine judgments (8:5, 11:19, 16:18). But before John can write these judgments down, a voice tells him to seal up the message. Two verses later, we find out why. The warnings (trumpets) had not prompted repentance in the hearers, and now judgment will be delayed no longer.

The concept of "sealing up" brings to mind the principle stated in Deuteronomy 29:29 and 2 Corinthians 12:4. The first of these reads: "The secret things belong to the LORD our God, but the things revealed belong to us and to our children forever, that we may follow all the words of this law." We may not have everything in the Bible we would like to have, but we have all that we need (2 Timothy 3:16-17, 2 Peter 1:3-4). At times we may wish for more details to satisfy our own curiosity, and at times we may wish for more details to convince others of the error of their doctrines. But the Bible is written in a way that demands a "leap of faith" on man's part. God's natural revelation (the physical creation) gives us sufficient evidence to see him without overpowering us into belief. If we have a heart to see, we will see, and if we do not have a heart to see, we will not see. The identical principle is involved with God's special revelation: the Bible. Spiritual hearts are enlightened and opened, while unspiritual hearts remain dark and closed. (See 1 Corinthians 1:18-31 and 2:12-15 for this principle.) 1 Corinthians 2:14 states it succinctly in this way:

The man without the Spirit does not accept the things that come
from the Spirit of God, for they are foolishness to him, and he
cannot understand them, because they are spiritually discerned.

Of course, in Revelation 10, the significance of the sealing is that no more warning is to be given (10:6). The sounding of the seventh trumpet does suggest the last trumpet at end of world, as we will see in 11:15. (See 1 Corinthians 15:52, 1 Thessalonians 4:16.) Before that occurs, however, John must eat the little scroll and keep on writing even after the seventh trumpet sounds.

> [8]*Then the voice that I had heard from heaven spoke to me once more: "Go, take the scroll that lies open in the hand of the angel who is standing on the sea and on the land."*
> [9]*So I went to the angel and asked him to give me the little scroll. He said to me, "Take it and eat it. It will turn your stomach sour, but in your mouth it will be as sweet as honey."* [10]*I took the little scroll from the angel's hand and ate it. It tasted as sweet as honey in my mouth, but when I had eaten it, my stomach turned sour.* [11]*Then I was told, "You must prophesy again about many peoples, nations, languages and kings."*

The significance of eating the scroll is that its message is to be completely digested. The symbolism is borrowed from Ezekiel's prophecy, and by reading Ezekiel the meaning in John's day is clear:

> *Then I looked, and I saw a hand stretched out to me. In it was a scroll, which he unrolled before me. On both sides of it were written words of lament and mourning and woe.*
> *And he said to me, "Son of man, eat what is before you, eat this scroll; then go and speak to the house of Israel." So I opened my mouth, and he gave me the scroll to eat.*
> *Then he said to me, "Son of man, eat this scroll I am giving you and fill your stomach with it." So I ate it, and it tasted as sweet as honey in my mouth.*
> *He then said to me: "Son of man, go now to the house of Israel and speak my words to them. You are not being sent to a people of obscure speech and difficult language, but to the house of Israel—not to many peoples of obscure speech and difficult language, whose words you cannot understand. Surely if I had sent you to them, they would have listened to you. But the house of Israel is not willing to listen to you because they are not willing to listen to me, for the whole house of Israel is hardened and obstinate. But I will make you as unyielding and hardened as they are." (Ezekiel 2:9-3:8)*

The sweet and sour combination has to do with God's word being precious (Psalm 119:103), even when the contents of that word are warnings and judgments. Any preacher who follows Paul's admonition to "correct, rebuke and encourage" (2 Timothy 4:2) will feel both the exhilaration of delivering the message of God and the burden of being uncompromising and unsentimental in its application. Paul himself felt the sting of having to challenge some of his closest friends, the elders of the church in Ephesus: "So be on your guard! Remember that for three years I never stopped warning each of you night and day with tears" (Acts 20:31).

The content of the little scroll was evidently the remainder of Revelation after the seventh trumpet (chapters 12-22), but this does not signal the completion of judgments. Revelation 10:11 constitutes a recommissioning of John to continue prophesying—God's message has not been fully delivered yet.

? What kinds of things in God's word are most pleasant and exciting to you? What kinds of things are most difficult for you to "swallow"? Are there any Biblical teachings that you tend to question? Do you feel negatively about any Biblical teachings? If yes, how have you tried to resolve your views and feelings?

Two Triumphant Witnesses (11:1-19)

> *11:1I was given a reed like a measuring rod and was told, "Go and measure the temple of God and the altar, and count the worshipers there. 2But exclude the outer court; do not measure it, because it has been given to the Gentiles. They will trample on the holy city for 42 months. 3And I will give power to my two witnesses, and they will prophesy for 1,260 days, clothed in sackcloth." 4These are the two olive trees and the two lampstands that stand before the Lord of the earth. 5If anyone tries to harm them, fire comes from their mouths and devours their enemies. This is how anyone who wants to harm them must die. 6These men have power to shut up the sky so that it will not rain during the time they are prophesying; and they have power to turn the waters into blood and to strike the earth with every kind of plague as often as they want.*

With the close of Revelation 11 comes the sounding of the seventh trumpet and the ending of the first half of the book. Before proceeding with the sounding of the seventh trumpet to end this first half of the prophecy, the temple is measured. This process shows God's protection of his people much like the "sealing" of chapter 7 did. Zechariah 2:1-5 uses similar figures to separate the holy from the profane:

> Then I looked up—and there before me was a man with a measuring line in his hand!
> I asked, "Where are you going?"
> He answered me, "To measure Jerusalem, to find out how wide and how long it is."
> Then the angel who was speaking to me left, and another angel came to meet him and said to him: "Run, tell that young man, 'Jerusalem will be a city without walls because of the great number of men and livestock in it. And I myself will be a wall of fire around it,' declares the Lord, 'and I will be its glory within.'"

The temple in the vision is physical (11:1), but it signifies the church as the true temple of God. Just as all of the redeemed were counted for protection in Revelation 7, the worshipers in the spiritual temple are carefully counted. They will be protected during the time of intense persecution about to be described. However, the outer court was not to receive protection. The OT temple complex was composed of many parts, including the inner temple and the courts surrounding it. The members of God's kingdom are composed of a spirit surrounded by a body. The lesson seems to be that Christians would be protected spiritually but not physically, which coincides with our observations in Chapter 7.

The "Gentiles" (persecutors) will be allowed to continue with their persecution of disciples for 42 months, the common designation of the period of persecution. As noted in Chapter 1, this is three and a half years or 1,260 days, and from the Book of Daniel, "a time, times, and half of a time." During this time of physical instability and uncertainty, God's preachers were anything but unstable or uncertain. The number two is used to denote their strength. They preached a powerful message (their message was like that of John the Baptist—"repent!") which yielded powerful results (11:3-6). They were clothed in sackcloth. They were called "olive trees" and "lampstands," which denoted a continual supply of the Spirit for their preaching. (See Zechariah 4 for the background of these figures.) The effects of their message remind us of the impact made by Moses and Elijah in the OT setting. Having a powerful influence is not related to the *time* when we live; it is related only to the *power* by which we live. The first century church, signified by the two witnesses, lived by the power of the Holy Spirit, and we have the opportunity to do the same.

> [7]*Now when they have finished their testimony, the beast that comes up from the Abyss will attack them, and overpower and kill them.* [8]*Their bodies will lie in the street of the great city, which is figuratively called Sodom and Egypt, where also their Lord was crucified.* [9]*For three and a half days men from every people, tribe, language and nation will gaze on their bodies and refuse them burial.* [10]*The inhabitants of the earth will gloat over them and will celebrate by sending each other gifts, because these two prophets had tormented those who live on the earth.*
>
> [11]*But after the three and a half days a breath of life from God entered them, and they stood on their feet, and terror struck those who saw them.* [12]*Then they heard a loud voice from heaven saying to them, "Come up here." And they went up to heaven in a cloud, while their enemies looked on.*
>
> [13]*At that very hour there was a severe earthquake and a tenth of the city collapsed. Seven thousand people were killed in the earthquake, and the survivors were terrified and gave glory to the God of heaven.*
>
> [14]*The second woe has passed; the third woe is coming soon.*

Once the testimony of the two witnesses is finished, the beast from the Abyss overpowers and kills them (11:7). A similar statement regarding the authority of Satan is found in 13:7: "He was given power to make war against the saints and to conquer them. And he was given authority over every tribe, people, language and nation." Satan had his way for a time, but his victory was to be short lived (11:11)! What we might call the first phase of the testimony of the early church was completed well before the end of the first century. Jesus said to preach the gospel to the ends of the earth, and Paul commented on the spread of the message by saying that it "has been proclaimed to every creature under heaven" (Colossians 1:23).

As the persecution intensified, it looked like the Christian cause had been snuffed out in defeat. However, such was not the case; the Christians had merely gone underground. The two witnesses lie slain in the streets of the "great city," which is Babylon, a figure for Rome in the book of Revelation (see 18:21). The great city is also figuratively called Sodom and Egypt and by implication, Jerusalem ("where their Lord was crucified"—11:8). What do these locations have in common with the persecution of the first century saints? All were known for persecution of the people of God in various centuries. The Roman Empire now embodied the savage rejection faced throughout history by God's finest.

The world's hatred of righteousness is vividly portrayed in 11:9-10. The venom spewed out toward disciples by all aspects of the world, including the religious world, is often *shocking* but hopefully never *surprising*. The apostle Peter wrote, "do not be surprised at the painful trial you are suffering, as though something strange were happening to you" (1 Peter 4:12). Jesus forewarned his apostles about the inevitability and intensity of persecution in chilling terms:

> *"If the world hates you, keep in mind that it hated me first. If you belonged to the world, it would love you as its own. As it is, you do not belong to the world, but I have chosen you out of the world. That is why the world hates you. Remember the words I spoke to you: 'No servant is greater than his master.' If they persecuted me, they will persecute you also. If they obeyed my teaching, they will obey yours also....*
>
> *"All this I have told you so that you will not go astray. They will put you out of the synagogue; in fact, a time is coming when anyone who kills you will think he is offering a service to God. They will do such things because they have not known the Father or me. I have told you this, so that when the time comes you will remember that I warned you." (John 15:18-20, 16:1-4)*

The Scriptures are quite clear about the subject of persecution. If we are not going to be surprised at the appearance of it in our lives, we need to understand some Biblical basics.[1] Much can be gained by looking up each of the passages listed below making careful notes about what is learned, and spending serious time in prayer about how to view and react to rejection.

The Progression of Persecution

    A. Jesus was widely acclaimed and accepted in the early stages of his ministry. However, his life and teaching eventually prompted those in the darkness to kill him.

B. Similarly, the early church experienced an initial acceptance followed by a progressive rejection. Study the following verses to see this progressive nature of persecution:
1. Early favor (Acts 2:46-47, 5:12-16).
2. Persecution of *apostles* in Jerusalem (Acts 4:16-20, 5:27-29, 40-42).
3. Persecution of *disciples* in Jerusalem (Acts 8:1-3).
4. Persecution in *other parts of the world* (Acts 17:5-8).
5. Persecution *everywhere* (Acts 28:21-22—they became the sect spoken against everywhere, the "cult" of their day!)

The Causes of Persecution

A. Family ties are threatened (Matthew 10:34-37).
B. False teachers and false teachings are threatened (1 Timothy 1:3-4, 2 Timothy 4:2-4).
C. Businesses or finances are threatened (Acts 19:23-34).
D. Worldly pleasures are threatened (1 Peter 4:3-4).

The Godly Responses to Persecution

A. Attitudes to possess:
1. Do not be surprised (1 Peter 4:12-16).
2. Realize that it could be worse (Hebrews 12:2-3).
3. Understand the power of suffering for Christ in drawing people to him (2 Corinthians 4:8-12, Colossians 1:24, 1 Peter 2:11-12).
4. Rejoice in the anticipation of God's reward (Matthew 5:10-12).
B. Actions to practice (1 Peter 3:13-17):
1. Do not give in to fear and back off of your convictions (1 Peter 3:14).
2. Continue to make Jesus the Lord of your life and to share your faith boldly (1 Peter 3:15).
3. Keep being gentle and respectful toward those who persecute you (1 Peter 3:16, Romans 12:17-21).
4. Make sure you are suffering for doing good and not for some sin (1 Peter 3:17).

5. Finally, just keep trusting God and doing what
   he says! (1 Peter 4:19).

In Revelation 11:11-13, we find that the supposed victory
against God's movement lasted only three-and-a-half days, a
short period compared to the three-and-a-half years of the persecution. (Keep in mind that these time periods are symbolic.)
A part of the reason that the Cause seemed defeated for such a
short time was the influence of the book of Revelation itself. It
was written to help the saints face the hardships with heart-
soaring faith and win the victory. This passage predicted that
very victory!

When Christianity seemed dead (especially to the world),
God breathed life back into it (11:11). The best cross-reference
in the Old Testament is without a doubt Ezekiel 37, a thrilling
vision of a valley of dry bones coming to life by the power of
God. In that context, the possibility of resurrecting Israel
seemed remote at best—even the prophet had little faith! Yet,
God has the power to do the unimaginable. And if he has that
sort of control over an entire nation, we are both faithless and
foolish to doubt what he can do in our individual lives.

*[15]The seventh angel sounded his trumpet, and there were
loud voices in heaven, which said:*

*"The kingdom of the world has become the kingdom of
our Lord and of his Christ,
and he will reign for ever and ever."*

*[16]And the twenty-four elders, who were seated on their thrones
before God, fell on their faces and worshiped God, [17]saying:*

*"We give thanks to you, Lord God Almighty,
    the One who is and who was,
because you have taken your great power
    and have begun to reign.
[18]The nations were angry;
    and your wrath has come.
The time has come for judging the dead,
    and for rewarding your servants the prophets
and your saints and those who reverence your name,
    both small and great—
and for destroying those who destroy the earth."*

[19]Then God's temple in heaven was opened, and within his temple was seen the ark of his covenant. And there came flashes of lightning, rumblings, peals of thunder, an earthquake and a great hailstorm.

This passage seems to indicate the last judgment, although a case can be made that it refers to the ultimate deliverance from the persecution under consideration. However, certain statements seem too final for that interpretation. Revelation 21 and 22 seem to refer to the end of time even more clearly (although some would disagree). If both passages do extend to the Judgment Day and eternity beyond, as seems most likely, the overall framework of Revelation becomes more obvious. Essentially, Revelation is divided into two sections which follow a similar path.

The first section (through Revelation 11) gives us the view of persecution as it originated and spread on earth. Then in Revelation 12, the beginning of the second section, we are taken behind the scenes and informed about the *roots* of the battle taking place on earth. These roots are none other than the age-old war with God and his angels against Satan and his angels (the demons). It's almost like a movie which leaves its current setting and goes back in time to show how the current events began. In section two of Revelation, we see these deeper origins of persecution and then God's intensifying judgments against the persecutors. In section one, he gave stern warnings in the form of the trumpets. In section two, he will pour out bowls of wrath and finish the job.

The sections are clearly related as they show two aspects of the same problem. Seen in this way, we come to realize that we humans have been caught up in a spiritual cataclysm of galactic proportions! We are playing out our parts on the stage of one little planet, but the battle is infinitely larger. God and Satan both have their angels and their allies, and disciples are God's allies on earth. Obviously, the allies of Satan are those in the pagan world. During the time of the Roman persecution, that evil empire comprised this alliance, particularly its leaders. Section two of Revelation will open up with the introduction of Satan and then will introduce his three primary allies in the Roman system. One by one, these allies will be destroyed, after which Satan himself will be destroyed. "Glory, glory, Hallelujah. Our God is marching on."

? As you studied the passages on the subject of persecution, which things struck your heart most? Does the idea of persecution, especially in your own life, tend to make you discouraged or determined? Explain your answer. When you hear things about the church or its leaders that concern you, do you first think "guilty" or "innocent"? Do you seek answers to your concerns?

10

▼

Behind the Scenes
REVELATION 12 AND 13

Now the plot thickens, and the battle intensifies. The book of Revelation, much like films and novels, employs the effective use of flashback. Much (probably most) of all that happens in one day in Revelation 12 flashes back to events of previous days, months or years. The present is tied inseparably to the past; one produces the other, and one is the product of the other. Persecution of God's people began long before Jesus walked the lonely path to Calvary. It was present throughout the OT period. From the Garden of Eden, all of humanity has been engaged in a holy war with staggering implications. Although we begin life in an innocent state, at some point we all volunteer for an army with a cold-blooded murderer as its leader. A small minority later figure out what a terrible choice they have made and join the righteous army led by the General of generals.

When this choice is made, literally all hell breaks loose. Satan hates righteousness in any person, but he hates the Author of righteousness most of all. This prince of the underworld has but one aim for his great intellect and great energy—to destroy everything sacred and everyone seeking sacred values. He never sleeps, he never relaxes, he never slows down; nothing deters him from his aim. He is not discouraged enough by defeats to lose heart or focus. He is truly amazing! Make no mistake about it, Satan is after you and me, but he can be defeated by any of us, if we learn his schemes and personality well. As Paul said, we must approach life with God's principles in hand, "in order that Satan might not outwit us. For we are not unaware of his schemes" (2 Corinthians 2:11). In the second half of this great spiritual drama, look for the satanic schemes designed to ensnare the soldiers of Christ. And then avoid them like the plagues they are!

Satan Cannot Prevail

Against the Birth of Jesus (12:1-6)

> *12:1A great and wondrous sign appeared in heaven: a woman clothed with the sun, with the moon under her feet and a crown of twelve stars on her head. 2She was pregnant and cried out in pain as she was about to give birth. 3Then another sign appeared in heaven: an enormous red dragon with seven heads and ten horns and seven crowns on his heads. 4His tail swept a third of the stars out of the sky and flung them to the earth. The dragon stood in front of the woman who was about to give birth, so that he might devour her child the moment it was born. 5She gave birth to a son, a male child, who will rule all the nations with an iron scepter. And her child was snatched up to God and to his throne. 6The woman fled into the desert to a place prepared for her by God, where she might be taken care of for 1,260 days.*

As we begin our look behind the scenes to the underlying spiritual causes of the persecution, we see an unusual pregnant woman. The description of her reminds us of the dream of Joseph in Genesis 37:9-11. In that account, Joseph's exaltation over his family is shown. In both scriptures, the twelve stars represent the twelve tribes of Israel (12:1). The Jewish nation was chosen to give birth to Jesus in a corporate sense, just as Mary was chosen in a specific sense (Luke 1:29-33, Galatians 4:4). The first messianic prophecy in the Bible is about the offspring of woman overcoming Satan (Genesis 3:15). When God established his covenant with the Jewish nation at Mount Sinai, he began speaking of his relationship with them as a marriage.[1]

The huge red dragon tried hard to kill this male child (12:3). Satan is pictured here as one with great wisdom (seven heads), great power (ten horns) and great authority (seven crowns). Perhaps you will recall that the number seven represents perfection and is normally descriptive of God or godly things. The application to Satan in this passage shows the capabilities he has. His tail sweeping stars out of heaven is a graphic portrayal of his tremendous power. (See Daniel 8:9-10 for the use of similar figures to describe a heathen political power.) Satan's purpose was to devour Jesus at his birth, and with the help of Herod, he devoured many children in his attempt to kill Jesus (Matthew 2:13-18). This male child was to rule the nations, as Psalm 2:9 foretold. In order to accept this rule, he ascended back to the Father's right hand, safe from the temptations of Satan.

Next, we are presented with one of those dreamlike changes in the vision (12:6). The OT woman (the Israelites) who gave birth to Jesus is now pictured as the NT woman (the church). The woman who flees into the wilderness must be understood as the church, since the previous verse showed the ascension of Jesus back to the Father. The lesson thus taught is a very important one. God's people are *one* regardless of the covenant under which they lived. While it is true that the majority of Israelites were never a part of the faithful remnant, it is also true that some of the finest men and women of faith ever to live were of that heritage. When we come into the kingdom, we join them as fellow servants of the Most High God. Consider the wording of Hebrews 12:22-23 (emphasis added):

> *But you have come to Mount Zion, to the heavenly Jerusalem, the city of the living God. You have come to thousands upon thousands of angels in joyful assembly, to the church of the firstborn, whose names are written in heaven. You have come to God, the judge of all men, to the spirits of righteous men made perfect.*

The latter reference is to those OT worthies who formed the foundation for God's new covenant kingdom. In the midst of another "wilderness wandering" in the desert of persecution for the prescribed duration (1,260 days), the NT people of God are carrying on with what these OT heroes started long ago!

This thought ushers in a related and important topic, namely the definition of the "kingdom of God." How would you define God's kingdom today? Most of us would answer simply "the church is God's kingdom." That statement contains the truth, but not *all* of the truth on the subject. Simply stated, the kingdom is where God's will is done by his subjects. If you recall the model prayer, Jesus taught us to pray "your kingdom come, your will be done on earth as it is in heaven" (Matthew 6:10). Those in heaven who have been delivered are as much a part of God's kingdom as we are. Did not Jesus say "There will be weeping there, and gnashing of teeth, when you see Abraham, Isaac and Jacob and all the prophets in the kingdom of God, but you yourselves thrown out"? (Luke 13:28). This passage, along with others like Hebrews 12:22-23, makes it clear that the kingdom includes the redeemed in heaven and the angels as well. (Such passages as Matthew 18:10 and Mark 13:32 give more reason to see the angels of God as part of the kingdom.)

What then should we say about the church? The most accurate way to define it is to describe it as the kingdom of God *on earth*. It is certainly the kingdom today, but even at that, it is not *all* of the kingdom. It is the kingdom on earth and clearly the kingdom foretold by the OT prophets in passages like Isaiah 2, Daniel 2 and Joel 2. Is the distinction we have made important? Yes, if you want to be able to harmonize all passages about the kingdom and to fully appreciate the kingdom of which you are now a part. Reread the Hebrews passage quoted above and grow in your appreciation of it.

Against Michael and His Angels (12:7-12)

> [7]*And there was war in heaven. Michael and his angels fought against the dragon, and the dragon and his angels fought back.* [8]*But he was not strong enough, and they lost their place in heaven.* [9]*The great dragon was hurled down—that ancient serpent called the devil, or Satan, who leads the whole world astray. He was hurled to the earth, and his angels with him.*
> [10]*Then I heard a loud voice in heaven say:*
>
> > *"Now have come the salvation and the power and the kingdom of our God,*
> > *and the authority of his Christ.*
> > *For the accuser of our brothers,*
> > *who accuses them before our God day and night,*
> > *has been hurled down.*
> > [11]*They overcame him*
> > *by the blood of the Lamb*
> > *and by the word of their testimony;*
> > *they did not love their lives so much*
> > *as to shrink from death.*
> > [12]*Therefore rejoice, you heavens*
> > *and you who dwell in them!*

But woe to the earth and the sea,
  because the devil has gone down to you!
He is filled with fury,
  because he knows that his time is short."

This section about Michael (12:7-9) is not a literal record of Satan's origin as a fallen angel, but rather a symbolic vision of Satan being unable to prevail against the spiritual forces of righteousness. Read Luke 10:18, John 12:31 and John 16:11 to see how his power was limited by God's. Concerning the origin of Satan, he must have been a leading angel at one time who was cast out of heaven because of rebellion. (See 1 Timothy 3:6, 2 Peter 2:4 and Jude 6 for related references.) Presumably Satan was the leader of those angels who sinned and were cast out. However, Revelation 12 is focusing on God's power over him generally as a way to encourage the saints. Most of us at one time or another will wonder why the devil seems to have such an amazing amount of power and why God allows such authority. He did not answer that question for the original readers of Revelation, but he did show them clearly who was really the Champion!

Michael is one of God's archangels (ruling angels). Gabriel, mentioned a number of times by name, apparently is another. The spiritual world is locked in a battle of good and evil, although we are basically unaware of it. For some mind-expanding reading to get in touch with the spiritual battle, you don't have to go to spiritual novels, although some of these are quite good.[2] Time spent reading and contemplating Revelation or related passages like Daniel 10 will make it abundantly clear that Satan really is alive and active on planet Earth!

In Revelation 12, Satan is described in several ways. He is the subtle serpent (12:9) who induced our oldest ancestors to sin in the Garden. He is the deceiver (12:9) who leads (nearly) the whole world astray by his white-washed lies, and the accuser (12:10) who would fill us with self doubt and God doubt. Some of us seem to be especially vulnerable to his accusations, always feeling guilty and "down on" ourselves. Some of us do not struggle much with having an accused conscience, but we are deceived about our spiritual condition. In the former case, we often feel guilty when we are not, and in the

latter case, we feel innocent when we are not. All such deception is from Satan, our great adversary.

According to 12:11, our early brothers and sisters were
victorious against Satan's deception. What were the keys to
their victory? One, they "overcame by the blood of the lamb."
Security in Christ is a precious Biblical doctrine which we need
to understand and live out daily. When we spend time studying books like Romans, we discover the difference between a
grace-centered walk with God and a performance-based walk—
one provides sustained motivation and the other does not.
Two, they overcame "by the word of their testimony" (12:11).
Sharing our faith daily is much more than a good idea; it is
essential if we want to keep a strong faith. Preaching the Word
builds faith, confidence and convictions. Three, they overcame by laying their lives on the line. Like their Lord, "they
died to make men free." They did not run from the battle,
even if the consequences were persecution and death. And
with a fury-driven enemy (12:12), these were inevitable.

Against the Church (12:13-17)

> [13]When the dragon saw that he had been hurled to the earth,
> he pursued the woman who had given birth to the male child.
> [14]The woman was given the two wings of a great eagle, so that
> she might fly to the place prepared for her in the desert, where
> she would be taken care of for a time, times and half a time,
> out of the serpent's reach. [15]Then from his mouth the serpent
> spewed water like a river, to overtake the woman and sweep
> her away with the torrent. [16]But the earth helped the woman
> by opening its mouth and swallowing the river that the dragon
> had spewed out of his mouth. [17]Then the dragon was enraged
> at the woman and went off to make war against the rest of her
> offspring—those who obey God's commandments and hold to
> the testimony of Jesus.

The church, depicted here as the woman, has become the
sole focus of Satanic attention (12:13). The Lord provides the
protection needed to stay out of Satan's reach. Satan spewed a
river of lies out to drown them in false doctrines, but they
refused to succumb. One of reasons the disciples did not fall
prey to these lies is that the earth swallowed them. In other
words, the world followed Satan's lies to the extent that the

Christians could see the fallacy and emptiness of living this way. Murder, drunkenness, incest, rape, lying, stealing, deceit, suicide—what clear-thinking person with a smattering of spiritual insight would volunteer for such? Give me love, joy and peace any day!

Since Satan was unable to destroy the church as a whole (the woman), he targeted individual Christians ("the rest of her offspring"—12:17). Little has changed through the centuries. Both God and Satan know that the battle is won or lost one person at a time. And they also both know that the battle is decided one day at a time. Whoever wins the daily battles will win the war. Consistency in life-style is a *huge* issue, because it builds character. For this reason, God gives us what could be called "the daily diet of a disciple." To defeat Satan in the same way our early brothers did, we need daily prayer (Luke 11:1-4, Psalm 5:1-3); daily Biblical nourishment (Acts 17:11); daily evangelism (Acts 17:16-17); and daily openness with our lives (James 5:16, Hebrews 3:12-13). Do these things and you cannot be defeated by anything Satan has at his disposal!

? Has this chapter helped you to see the unity of purpose between the OT people of God and the church? Do you understand more about the nature of the kingdom of God? (If not, keep studying.) How are you doing with the "daily diet of a disciple?" Which of the four areas do you most need to improve? Will you?

Satan's Two Allies: The Beasts

The Beast from the Sea (13:1-10)

> [13:1]And the dragon stood on the shore of the sea.
>
> And I saw a beast coming out of the sea. He had ten horns and seven heads, with ten crowns on his horns, and on each head a blasphemous name. [2]The beast I saw resembled a leopard, but had feet like those of a bear and a mouth like that of a lion. The dragon gave the beast his power and his throne and great authority. [3]One of the heads of the beast seemed to have had a fatal wound, but the fatal wound had been healed. The whole world was astonished and followed the beast. [4]Men worshiped the dragon because he had given authority to the beast, and they also worshiped the beast and asked, "Who is like the beast? Who can make war against him?"
>
> [5]The beast was given a mouth to utter proud words and blasphemies and to exercise his authority for forty-two months.

⁶He opened his mouth to blaspheme God, and to slander his name and his dwelling place and those who live in heaven. ⁷He was given power to make war against the saints and to conquer them. And he was given authority over every tribe, people, language and nation. ⁸All inhabitants of the earth will worship the beast—all whose names have not been written in the book of life belonging to the Lamb that was slain from the creation of the world.
    ⁹He who has an ear, let him hear.

¹⁰If anyone is to go into captivity,
    into captivity he will go.
If anyone is to be killed
    with the sword, with the sword he will be killed.

This calls for patient endurance and faithfulness on the part of the saints.

Revelation 12 not only introduces us to the deeper battle between the devil and Christ; it assures us that the war has already been won. With that assurance in mind, reading the account of Satan's allies and how they operate is not so fearful. The first beast arises out of the sea (13:1), the sea of humanity from which world powers come. John seems to borrow from Daniel 7 in this description.

Daniel said: "In my vision at night I looked, and there before me were the four winds of heaven churning up the great sea. Four great beasts, each different from the others, came up out of the sea.
    "The first was like a lion, and it had the wings of an eagle. I watched until its wings were torn off and it was lifted from the ground so that it stood on two feet like a man, and the heart of a man was given to it.
    "And there before me was a second beast, which looked like a bear. It was raised up on one of its sides, and it had three ribs in its mouth between its teeth. It was told, 'Get up and eat your fill of flesh!'
    "After that, I looked, and there before me was another beast, one that looked like a leopard. And on its back it had four wings like those of a bird. This beast had four heads, and it was given authority to rule.

> *"After that, in my vision at night I looked, and there before me was a fourth beast—terrifying and frightening and very powerful. It had large iron teeth; it crushed and devoured its victims and trampled underfoot whatever was left. It was different from all the former beasts, and it had ten horns." (Daniel 7:2-7)*

Daniel goes on to describe the beasts as four kingdoms, the fourth of which was the same as in Daniel 2—none other than the Roman Empire (Daniel 7:17, 23). From the description that follows, we will see that the beast is an aspect of Rome, namely the political power represented by the emperor. He has the authority of Satan himself. (Compare 12:3 with 13:1 to see the tie-in.) The blasphemous names were the claims of deity by the emperors, especially Domitian.

Note that in Revelation, one of the heads of the beast seemed to have a fatal wound, but had healed (13:3). This most likely refers to Nero who reigned from 54-68 AD and was the first of the Roman persecutors. The "healing" would have been the resumed persecution under Domitian (81-96 AD). Just as John the Baptist was the Elijah of prophecy (Matthew 17:10-12), having come in the "spirit and power" of Elijah (Luke 1:17), Domitian had come in the spirit and power of Nero. The figure may be a play on what was called the "Nero Redivivus Myth," the idea that Nero would return alive as the leader of the Parthians against Rome.

The mission of this sea beast (13:5) was to utter proud words and blasphemies (demanding worship as deity) and to bring about persecution against the saints for 42 months (the standard designation for the period of persecution). The result of his mission against heaven and spiritual inhabitants of earth was that everyone worshiped him except those written in the book of life (13:8). The emperor was exalted by the nations because of Rome's contributions to the world. He was feared because of the military power at his disposal ("who can make war against him?" in 13:4).

In the mind of God, Jesus was slain before the world was created (13:8, and see 1 Peter 1:20) as an atonement for sins, but only a few had opened their eyes to see the plan. What a sad commentary on the blindness and lostness of humanity!

The message in 13:10 is that the just punishment of the enemies of God's people will definitely come. This certainty gives hope to the saints and also reminds them not to give in to the temptation to retaliate ("this calls for patient endurance and faithfulness"—13:10). (See God's promise in 2 Thessalonians 1:6 to "pay back trouble to those who trouble you.") God is "sifting out the hearts of men before his judgment seat." No one will get past the justice of God. Either it will be satisfied in our acceptance of his slain Son, or it will be satisfied in a manner horrible beyond comprehension:

> He will punish those who do not know God and do not obey the gospel of our Lord Jesus. They will be punished with everlasting destruction and shut out from the presence of the Lord and from the majesty of his power. (2 Thessalonians 1:8-9)

The Beast from the Earth (13:11-18)

> [11]Then I saw another beast, coming out of the earth. He had two horns like a lamb, but he spoke like a dragon. [12]He exercised all the authority of the first beast on his behalf, and made the earth and its inhabitants worship the first beast, whose fatal wound had been healed. [13]And he performed great and miraculous signs, even causing fire to come down from heaven to earth in full view of men. [14]Because of the signs he was given power to do on behalf of the first beast, he deceived the inhabitants of the earth. He ordered them to set up an image in honor of the beast who was wounded by the sword and yet lived. [15]He was given power to give breath to the image of the first beast, so that it could speak and cause all who refused to worship the image to be killed. [16]He also forced everyone, small and great, rich and poor, free and slave, to receive a mark on his right hand or on his forehead, [17]so that no one could buy or sell unless he had the mark, which is the name of the beast or the number of his name.
>
> [18]This calls for wisdom. If anyone has insight, let him calculate the number of the beast, for it is man's number. His number is 666.

Now we are introduced to the second ally of Satan, the beast arising out of the earth (13:11). Back in 12:16, the earth had swallowed the lies of Satan, and this beast not only believed the lies but spread them forcefully. The identity of this beast is not difficult to determine because his description in the text is very specific. He had the appearance of a lamb, a religious figure. We are reminded of Jesus' words in Matthew 7:15: "Watch out for false prophets. They come to you in sheep's clothing, but inwardly they are ferocious wolves." Later in Revelation, this beast is clearly identified as the "false prophet" who accompanied the other beast (16:13, 19:20, 20:10).

This second beast spoke like the dragon, for he was an agent of Satan (see 2 Corinthians 11:3). As such, he enforced worship of the emperor (the first beast). He was the second of three allies of Satan, all three of which most likely represented different aspects of Rome. Beast number one signified political Rome, beast number two was religious Rome, and the third ally was worldly, materialistic Rome (introduced in Revelation 17 as the prostitute). The religious arm of Rome set up images and demanded worship of the emperor. The specific agency of the empire was called the *Commune* or *Concillia*, an official body set up in Asia Minor to enforce emperor worship. Roman subjects had to burn a pinch of incense and say "Caesar is Lord" in order to stay in the good graces of the government. Otherwise, persecution reigned supreme. Secular history confirms that the consequences listed in this passage were a reality for Jesus' disciples.

Two relevant passages shed light on Satan's ability to dupe people to fall for such outlandish schemes. Read them and compare their principles to the Roman situation under consideration.

> *The coming of the lawless one will be in accordance with the work of Satan displayed in all kinds of counterfeit miracles, signs and wonders, and in every sort of evil that deceives those who are perishing. They perish because they refused to love the truth and so be saved. For this reason God sends them a powerful delusion so that they will believe the lie and so that all will be condemned who have not believed the truth but have delighted in wickedness. (2 Thessalonians 2:9-12)*

> *For such men are false apostles, deceitful workmen, masquerading as apostles of Christ. And no wonder, for Satan himself masquerades as an angel of light. It is not surprising, then, if his servants masquerade as servants of righteousness. Their end will be what their actions deserve. (2 Corinthians 11:13-15)*

In 13:16-17, we find mention of the "mark of the beast." An entire volume could be written describing all the outlandish interpretations given to this mark. Some otherwise intelligent people have been known to identify it with things like credit cards and social security numbers! How would such figures have helped persecuted disciples 1,900 years ago? The very idea of applying this mark to something so far removed from their problems, needs, and historical setting is preposterous.

Now that we know what the mark was not, what was it? Back in 7:3 the 144,000 (all of the redeemed) were sealed on their foreheads, denoting their intellectual facilities. Here in Revelation 13, the mark was applied to their foreheads (minds) and hands (service). Thus, one had to accept the emperor's claims of deity in both mind and action. Compare this to God's admonition to the Israelites to accept his teaching into their lives completely: "Fix these words of mine in your hearts and minds; tie them as symbols on your hands and bind them on your foreheads" (Deuteronomy 11:18). Roman subjects at some point may have had to carry some sort of certificate showing that they had met the requirements of emperor worship. But the mark itself seems to be symbolic of accepting the emperor's claims and commands regarding his deity.

Revelation 13 closes with an ominous statement about the beast's number, 666. Again, enormous amounts of paper and ink have been used in writing about the identity of Mr. 666! Virtually every world leader has been so identified, as well as multitudes of other individuals. Again we must ask what such interpretations would have meant to those in the early centuries dying for their faith? "Two thousand years from now, in a far away land not yet discovered, a certain liberal politician will become president of his country and..." A good beginning for a fairy tale perhaps, but not in the least related to the book of Revelation!

The beast has already been identified as political Rome, represented primarily by the emperor. By the use of the number, the first readers were to learn something about him which would help them in their situation. What might the intended lesson have been? If you recall from reading Chapter 1 about interpretation principles, the number "six" was the superstitious number to the Jewish mind because it fell short of the perfect number "seven." Six was an evil, sinister number and

Domitian was evil raised to the highest power. Verse 18 tells us that 666 was *"man's"* number, not simply *a* man's number. In other words, all humans fell far short of measuring up to God, and the emperor was no better. Their best-laid plans would be destroyed in the blink of an eye by him. God is so far ahead of them that any comparison was a waste of time. He was 777 (perfection upon perfection upon perfection) while they were 666 (failure upon failure upon failure).

Other possibilities may be feasible (or even *slightly* more accurate!), but we know who the beast was and we know who he wasn't—God! Therefore, why fear him? Surely this must have been the lesson to be gained from the figures used in the verse.

Although the beast is clearly identified as the Roman empire in the context of Revelation, other "beastlike" figures have appeared during the centuries since then. While we don't need to be searching for the one person in history who matches up with 666, we need to realize many will come in the same spirit. Domitian was not the first nor the last powerful ruler to oppose the people of God. While Hitler was not the beast of Revelation, he was like him, and he has the same end. The same could be said for the oppressive rulers in our own day. When Christians start dying in nations violently opposed to Christianity, this realization will become much more significant.

Now back to the conclusion of Revelation 13. Yes, Satan had his allies, but just as he could not even deal with God's archangel, much less God himself, his allies did not stand a chance either. They are introduced here in this chapter, only to be destroyed in hell in a later chapter!

? How serious do you think the issue of false religion is? Do you struggle with the concept that only those who accurately do the will of God are going to be saved? If yes, will you spend some time reading and meditating on the following passages? Matthew 7:13-14, 21; Acts 20:28-31; Romans 16:17-18; 2 Corinthians 11:13-15; Galatians 1:6-9; 1 Timothy 4:1-3; 2 Timothy 4:1-4.

11

▼

Last Call for Repentance
REVELATION 14

After the reader has been taken behind the scenes to understand the deeper nature of the spiritual battle, Satan and two of his allies are then introduced. Before proceeding with their final defeat, God issues a last call for repentance in Revelation 14. Sadly, that call was ignored, which leads into chapter 15 where repentance is no longer possible. God's last plagues will be poured out of the bowls as his wrath is completed (15:1). Revelation 14 thus constitutes his last warning before Rome's demise becomes reality. The first segment of this last call is another description of the 144,000. Following this description will be the warnings and the consequences for not heeding them. All through the book, God alternately encourages the righteous and warns the unrighteous (which also encourages the righteous!). Our present passage is a good example of both approaches.

The 144,000 Revisited (14:1-5)

14:1Then I looked, and there before me was the Lamb, standing on Mount Zion, and with him 144,000 who had his name and his Father's name written on their foreheads. 2And I heard a sound from heaven like the roar of rushing waters and like a loud peal of thunder. The sound I heard was like that of harpists playing their harps. 3And they sang a new song before the throne and before the four living creatures and the elders. No one could learn the song except the 144,000 who had been redeemed from the earth. 4These are those who did not defile themselves with women, for they kept themselves pure. They follow the Lamb wherever he goes. They were purchased from among men and offered as firstfruits to God and the Lamb. 5No lie was found in their mouths; they are blameless.

Each of the three main visions in Revelation 14 is set off by a statement such as "then I looked" (14:1, 6, 14). The first look revealed Jesus on Mount Zion with the 144,000 who were initially introduced in Revelation 7. In the former passage, they were sealed for protection, and in the latter, their character and their victory are described more fully. Their spirits must have been lifted tremendously as they read about God's view of them.

When John received the vision, he was as impressed with the sounds as with the sights. Great music filled the air, loud and melodious. The 144,000 joined voices with the four living creatures and elders whose praise to God first was seen (and heard) back in Revelation 4 and 5. They are singing their new song before God's throne, which demonstrates their victory (14:3). In Revelation 7, when they reached the throne, they were simply a great innumerable multitude who no longer needed to be numbered for sealing and protection. In our present passage, they are still numbered—even before the throne—showing perhaps that all the disciples could (and should) make it through the trials and tribulations they were facing at the hand of Rome.

Mount Zion (14:1) is a figure for God's total kingdom, in heaven and on earth (Hebrews 12:22-24). No one besides the 144,000 could learn this new song, for it was spiritually discerned (1 Corinthians 2:14). The unspiritual simply do not comprehend spiritual truths. If they do not have a heart desirous of understanding, they cannot understand. But those who have been redeemed by the blood of the Lamb thrill to sing redemption's sweet song!

The moral character of the redeemed is described in 14:4-5. They were not immoral, meaning primarily that they were spiritually pure. Of course, this purity presupposes that they were sexually pure in a physical sense as well. The Bible makes more references to the marriage analogy between God and his people than most realize.)[1] Just thinking about being married to God is heart-thrilling, and grasping some of the deeper lessons involved is life-changing. Paul understood the concept well when he wrote: "I am jealous for you with a godly jealousy. I promised you to one husband, to Christ, so that I might present you as a pure virgin to him" (2 Corinthians 11:2).

Another characteristic of the 144,000 is their allegiance to the Lamb (14:4). They follow him wherever he goes (see John 10:4, 1 John 2:6). Now that statement is a pregnant one indeed! Jesus goes many directions. He set an example of total self-denial, the most difficult of all decisions to make and carry out on a daily basis. He spoke the truth to those who were anxious to hear it and to those who absolutely hated to hear it. He worked late into the nights in order to meet the needs of others and then arose before dawn to spend time in prayer with his Father. He never compromised his convictions, even when Golgotha was the consequence.

Much more could be said about the life he lived. John was quite accurate in his assessment of this reality when he wrote: "Jesus did many other things as well. If every one of them were written down, I suppose that even the whole world would not have room for the books that would be written" (John 21:25). And yet the 144,000 lived lives characteristic of the Lamb's! Such Jesus-imitating lives produce unbelievable security:

> "My sheep listen to my voice; I know them, and they follow me. I give them eternal life, and they shall never perish; no one can snatch them out of my hand. My Father, who has given them to me, is greater than all; no one can snatch them out of my Father's hand." (John 10:27-29)

The depth of security we feel deep down in our heart of hearts demonstrates just how well we are following the Lamb wherever he goes.

The 144,000 were purchased by the blood of Christ to be firstfruits to God and the Lamb (14:4). In the Old Testament, devoting the first part of the agricultural harvest to God was a way of recognizing that all belonged to him in actuality. His reward for such recognition was to bless the remainder of the harvest in an abundant way. (See Deuteronomy 26:1-11.) This concept is applied spiritually in a number of ways. Jesus was called the firstfruits of the dead (1 Corinthians 15:20, 23), which guaranteed our resurrection from the dead. Paul called the first converts in Asia and Achaia the firstfruits (Romans 16:5, 1 Corinthians 16:15—King James Version). Obviously, God blessed these areas with an abundant continuing harvest of souls.

By way of practical application, what lesson does God want us to gain from the firstfruits analogy? Whoever and wherever we are, he wants us to dedicate ourselves to him in such a way that the salvation of many souls follows our conversion. We must view ourselves as the beginning point in many life situations: in our family, our school, our classroom, our neighborhood, our workplace, our groups and clubs, etc. If we are true firstfruits, our being harvested should guarantee a subsequent harvest of many others in our sphere of influence.

The concluding description of the 144,000 is found in 14:5. They are truthful, refusing to lie. Certainly the lie in this context is the lie that Caesar is Lord. But if these early disciples refused to bend the truth to save their lives, they must have been completely honest in all other areas as well. (Since they were following the Lamb in any direction he went, they could not have done otherwise!) True disciples tell the truth and want to hear the truth, even when it hurts. In our day of people pleasing, conflict avoidance and subtle rationalization, we would do well to imitate those described in such heroic terms here.

? How well do your spiritual characteristics match up with those of the 144,000? How much inner security do you feel in your relationship with Christ? What do you need to do about being "firstfruits" in your sphere of influence? What will you do?

Three Angels with Messages (14:6-13)

> [6]Then I saw another angel flying in midair, and he had the eternal gospel to proclaim to those who live on the earth—to every nation, tribe, language and people. [7]He said in a loud voice, "Fear God and give him glory, because the hour of his judgment has come. Worship him who made the heavens, the earth, the sea and the springs of water."
>
> [8]A second angel followed and said, "Fallen! Fallen is Babylon the Great, which made all the nations drink the maddening wine of her adulteries."
>
> [9]A third angel followed them and said in a loud voice: "If anyone worships the beast and his image and receives his mark on the forehead or on the hand, [10]he, too, will drink of the wine of God's fury, which has been poured full strength into the cup of his wrath. He will be tormented with burning sulfur in the presence of the holy angels and of the Lamb. [11]And the smoke of their torment rises for ever and ever. There is no rest

> *day or night for those who worship the beast and his image,
> or for anyone who receives the mark of his name." ¹²This calls
> for patient endurance on the part of the saints who obey God's
> commandments and remain faithful to Jesus.*
>   *¹³Then I heard a voice from heaven say, "Write: Blessed
> are the dead who die in the Lord from now on."*
>   *"Yes," says the Spirit, "they will rest from their labor, for
> their deeds will follow them."*

The three angels make pronouncements relating to the
last call to repentance. The first calls all on earth to fear God
and give him glory; the second shows that Rome is certain to
fall; and the third describes the eternal consequences of not
repenting. This first angel flies in midair for those from every
possible background to hear him. The gospel is for all, as the
Great Commission makes clear. The admonition to fear God
shows how repentance and faith must begin (14:7). As the
Proverb writer put it: "The fear of the LORD is the beginning of
knowledge" (Proverbs 1:7). When there is "no fear of God
before their eyes" (Romans 3:18), the whole world ends up
enmeshed in sin.

The second angel announces the fall of Babylon the Great
(14:8). "Babylon" calls to mind that wicked city in the OT
period responsible for unthinkable brutality against the people
of God. Here Babylon represented imperial Rome in its evil,
as the literal Babylon suggested the evils brought on the Jews
in their captivity. Babylon is described as the mother of prostitutes in 17:5, signifying the worldliness of Rome. The wording in 14:8 shows the city as *already* fallen to emphasize its
certainty. Back in Jeremiah 51:8, the prophet predicted something similar regarding the fall of actual Babylon decades before it occurred: "Suddenly Babylon has fallen and been broken" (NASV, which is more accurate here in translating the
verb tense). Therefore, it is useless to hold on to a disappear-
ing life-style. God has spoken, and it will be done!

The third angel (14:9-12) shows the horrifying consequences
of emperor worship. Those who followed this blasphemous practice would drink the wine of God's fury, and it would not be
watered down. Drinking the adulterous wine of Rome's worldliness (14:8) guaranteed that the latter wine would be drunk as
well. Hell, with its fire and brimstone, would be the ultimate
destiny of those who received the mark of the beast (14:10-11).

Reading passages describing hell always raises the question of how literally the descriptions are to be taken. No more literally than the gates of pearl and the streets of gold in heaven. However, if the descriptions of heaven are only an inadequate attempt to portray the wonders of it, we would have to make a similar assumption regarding hell. Because of our human limitations, we cannot fully understand the magnificence of heaven; and because of those same limitations, we cannot fully grasp the horrors of hell.

This passage of Scripture concludes with an admonition and a blessing directed toward God's children (14:12). Perseverance had to be maintained in the midst of the storm. Nothing demonstrates faith quite like holding on to God when Satan is trying hard to stir our doubts into roaring flames. Following Abraham and "hoping against hope" says "I love you" to God in a very special way. When we follow the admonition to persevere, the beatitude of 14:13 is God's reward—rest from our labor. To the tired soldier, the prospect of rest is a welcome one. Jesus promised rest for our *souls* in Matthew 11:29, but the rest for everything else does not come until we reach eternity! The person who lives out the mission of Jesus will have some deeds following them into eternity (in the form of saved souls). Just as bad deeds follow us into the Judgment Day (1 Timothy 5:24), so do good ones. Many years ago I heard a statement that encapsulates this concept succinctly: "Never give up your life for anything that death can take away." Well said. For this principle let us live, and with this principle let us die!

Two Sickles and Harvest (14:14-20)

> [14]*I looked, and there before me was a white cloud, and seated on the cloud was one "like a son of man" with a crown of gold on his head and a sharp sickle in his hand.* [15]*Then another angel came out of the temple and called in a loud voice to him who was sitting on the cloud, "Take your sickle and reap, because the time to reap has come, for the harvest of the earth is ripe."* [16]*So he who was seated on the cloud swung his sickle over the earth, and the earth was harvested.*
>
> [17]*Another angel came out of the temple in heaven, and he too had a sharp sickle.* [18]*Still another angel, who had charge of the fire, came from the altar and called in a loud voice to*

*him who had the sharp sickle, "Take your sharp sickle and
gather the clusters of grapes from the earth's vine, because its
grapes are ripe." [19]The angel swung his sickle on the earth,
gathered its grapes and threw them into the great winepress
of God's wrath. [20]They were trampled in the winepress outside
the city, and blood flowed out of the press, rising as high as
the horses' bridles for a distance of 1,600 stadia.*

The remainder of Revelation 14 deals with the promise of
a harvest of the earth. Two sickles are the instruments of this
harvest. The first is wielded by one "like a son of man"—Jesus
(1:12-16, Daniel 7:13-14)—and the second by an angel from
the temple. The key question is what the difference is between
the two harvest symbols. Are they both simply two aspects of
the same harvest, or does one picture the harvest of the righteous and other the harvest of the wicked? Either way, the
purpose of the vision is to show the absolute certainty of an
ultimate reckoning before God. This final call to repentance
must take this certainty into account.

The sickle figure is used in Joel 3:13 in connection with a
harvest of judgment against Tyre and Sidon. "Swing the sickle,
for the harvest is ripe. Come, trample the grapes, for the
winepress is full and the vats overflow—so great is their wickedness!" In Mark 4:26-29, the sickle harvests those in the kingdom of God. Therefore the sickle figure could be used in either type of harvest. It seems most likely that the first sickle
represents the harvest of the righteous in the spirit of Matthew 3:12, which reads: "His winnowing fork is in his hand,
and he will clear his threshing floor, gathering his wheat into
the barn and burning up the chaff with unquenchable fire."

The second sickle brings about a harvest of ripe grapes, as
the sins of the wicked had reached the point that harvest was
inevitable. In context, the judgment is representative of the
destruction of the evil persecuting empire rather than the Judgment Day which will be reached later, and will end with a lake
of fire rather than a winepress. However, a temporal judgment
insures a final Judgment. The two concepts are closely related,
both representing the justice of God that must be met. In 14:20,
symbolism is obviously demanded by the very nature of the
terms used. Those who would reduce Revelation to literalism

will have great difficulty fitting a two-hundred-mile river of blood into Palestine! The point is that God will be with the righteous and will be against the wicked. When God's judgment (any judgment) against the wicked seems long in coming, we would do well to remember these words of Peter:

> *But do not forget this one thing, dear friends: With the Lord a day is like a thousand years, and a thousand years are like a day. The Lord is not slow in keeping his promise, as some understand slowness. He is patient with you, not wanting anyone to perish, but everyone to come to repentance.*
>
> *But the day of the Lord will come like a thief. The heavens will disappear with a roar; the elements will be destroyed by fire, and the earth and everything in it will be laid bare.*
>
> *Since everything will be destroyed in this way, what kind of people ought you to be? You ought to live holy and godly lives. (2 Peter 3:8-11)*

The latter part of Revelation 14 provided the basis for the wording of the heart-moving song which reminds us of the certainty of God's judgments: "He is trampling out the vintage where the grapes of wrath are stored." The theme of judgment is a recurring one all of the way through Scripture. It is built into the heart of the universe, and all men have some sense of its reality. For that reason, the wicked described in Romans 1:32 seek the sinful involvement of others, wistfully hoping against hope that there will be safety in numbers:

> *Although they know God's righteous decree that those who do such things deserve death, they not only continue to do these very things but also approve of those who practice them.*

The sense of impending judgment is also evidenced in man's fear of death. Such a fear is not so much the fear of the unknown as is often assumed; it is due more to the innate fear of the Unknown (God)! While God wants his children to be motivated primarily out of love and appreciation for him, he also intends that we keep a healthy fear of judgment. The book of Revelation certainly provides us with some unforgettable images to prompt such a mindset.

? Regarding the subject of perseverance, what types of temptations and problems make you want to give up? Can you think of temptations which once caused you a lot of struggle but which you have gained significant victories over now? Spend time visualizing your present temptation challenges being overcome. Do you have a correct fear of judgment or an incorrect fear? Explain.

12

▼

Pour Out the Bowls
REVELATION 15 AND 16

At this point in Revelation, you may be wondering how much judgment can possibly remain! But there is much yet to come. The repeated emphases on God's punishment of the wicked makes it clear just how much reassurance the persecuted saints needed. When everything in sight seems to demonstrate the presence and power of Satan, everything in faith had to demonstrate the opposite. To that end God provided multitudinous promises of sin's destruction. And now, with John, let us open our eyes and hearts to "another great and marvelous sign."

The Preparation (15:1-8)

15:1 I saw in heaven another great and marvelous sign: seven angels with the seven last plagues—last, because with them God's wrath is completed. 2And I saw what looked like a sea of glass mixed with fire and, standing beside the sea, those who had been victorious over the beast and his image and over the number of his name. They held harps given them by God 3and sang the song of Moses the servant of God and the song of the Lamb:

> *"Great and marvelous are your deeds,*
> *Lord God Almighty.*
> *Just and true are your ways,*
> *King of the ages.*
> *4Who will not fear you, O Lord,*
> *and bring glory to your name?*
> *For you alone are holy.*
> *All nations will come*
> *and worship before you,*
> *for your righteous acts have been revealed."*

*⁵After this I looked and in heaven the temple, that is, the tab-
ernacle of the Testimony, was opened. ⁶Out of the temple came
the seven angels with the seven plagues. They were dressed in
clean, shining linen and wore golden sashes around their
chests. ⁷Then one of the four living creatures gave to the seven
angels seven golden bowls filled with the wrath of God, who
lives for ever and ever. ⁸And the temple was filled with smoke
from the glory of God and from his power, and no one could
enter the temple until the seven plagues of the seven angels
were completed.*

Revelation 15 begins a new cycle, forming an introduction to the bowls of wrath in the next chapter. The mention
of a great and marvelous sign in 15:1 is very similar to 12:1.
Both passages were obviously introducing something of special significance. The seven last plagues mark the culmina-
tion of God's wrath, a reference to the final defeat of the persecuting Roman system.

The sea of glass was mentioned back in 4:6 to indicate the
transcendence of God and the subsequent separation from
mortals. Here in 15:2, we see two differences. One, those who
have passed through the persecution in victory are now standing *on* the sea (NASV). The sea is still there, but they are now
drawn close to God through their perseverance. Two, the sea
of glass has fire mixed in with it. The fire is likely an indication of the trials through which they had emerged victori-
ously. 1 Peter 1:7 is an excellent reference for this idea:

*These have come so that your faith—of greater worth than
gold, which perishes even though refined by fire—may be
proved genuine and may result in praise, glory and honor when
Jesus Christ is revealed.*

Next in the vision comes the song of Moses and the Lamb
(15:3-4). Redemption's song is comprised of two choruses, an
OT chorus and a NT chorus. Even though we have two different covenants involved, both are from God, and one builds
upon the other. The new is in the old concealed, and the old
is in the new revealed. As was mentioned in the comments
about Revelation 12, the people of God are unified by the
blood of the Lamb. When he died, it was for the sins of those
who lived before and after the cross (Hebrews 9:15, Romans

3:25). The Israelites sang their song of deliverance when they marched through the Red Sea and were delivered from Egyptian persecution (Exodus 15). The persecuted in our present passage sang their song when they had passed from death to life and were delivered from Roman persecution. The phrases in the song itself come from a number of OT passages, particularly Psalms.

The angels introduced in 15:1 now come out from the very presence of God in the temple with the seven last plagues. "Clouds and thick darkness surround him; righteousness and justice are the foundation of his throne. Fire goes before him and consumes his foes on every side" (Psalm 97:2-3). In 8:3-5, judgment came from the altar based on saint's prayers, but now it comes from God very directly. Once the angels receive the plagues, smoke fills the temple, prohibiting entrance by anyone. In the OT setting, priests could enter the temple to offer intercession, thus intervening to stop a plague. (See Numbers 16:42-48 for an excellent example of Aaron being able to cause a terrible plague to cease.) But in 15:8, nothing or no one could stop the inevitable satisfaction of the justice of God. Rome was doomed.

It is a sobering thought that we can sin away the day of God's grace. He offers amazing grace, to be sure, but he does have a limit—just ask the people who begged Noah to let them into the ark when the flood waters began rising. We should all take with the utmost seriousness our own need to repent, especially in areas which should have changed long ago. It is a dangerous thing to test God's outer extremities of grace! Consider Proverbs 1:23-31:

> "If you had responded to my rebuke,
>   I would have poured out my heart to you
>   and made my thoughts known to you.
> But since you rejected me when I called
>   and no one gave heed when I stretched out my hand,
> since you ignored all my advice
>   and would not accept my rebuke,
> I in turn will laugh at your disaster;
>   I will mock when calamity overtakes you—
> when calamity overtakes you like a storm,
>   when disaster sweeps over you like a whirlwind,
>   when distress and trouble overwhelm you.

Then they will call to me but I will not answer;
*   they will look for me but will not find me.*
Since they hated knowledge
*   and did not choose to fear the LORD,*
since they would not accept my advice
*   and spurned my rebuke,*
they will eat the fruit of their ways
*   and be filled with the fruit of their schemes. "*

? How do you feel about the idea of sinning away the day of God's grace? Are you taking seriously your need to repent in every area of your life that is not like Jesus? Is there any area in which you are resisting repentance? Explain the difference between getting convicted and developing a conviction. Which one of these conditions do you find yourself in most often?

As we said in reference to the trumpets of Revelation 8 and 9, a number of similarities exist between the trumpets and the bowls. Their contents are closely related with woes brought upon nature and man, signified with much symbolism from Egyptian plagues. They both end with a type of judgment scene. But there are marked differences in the two series. The trumpets were calls to repentance, whereas the bowls are judgments after the hope of repentance is past. The trumpets were partial in their effects, affecting only one-third of whatever they struck. The bowls were final, affecting the whole target. The trumpets did not reach man until the fifth in the series, but the bowls fall upon man from the first.

Nature Affected by the First Bowl (16:1-9)

16:1 Then I heard a loud voice from the temple saying to the seven angels, "Go, pour out the seven bowls of God's wrath on the earth."
2 The first angel went and poured out his bowl on the land, and ugly and painful sores broke out on the people who had the mark of the beast and worshiped his image.
3 The second angel poured out his bowl on the sea, and it turned into blood like that of a dead man, and every living thing in the sea died.
4 The third angel poured out his bowl on the rivers and springs of water, and they be became blood. 5 Then I heard the angel in charge of the waters say:
"You are just in these judgments,
*   you who are and who were, the Holy One,*

because you have so judged;
⁶for they have shed the blood of your saints and prophets,
   and you have given them blood to drink as they deserve."
⁷And I heard the altar respond:
   "Yes, Lord God Almighty,
   true and just are your judgments."
   ⁸The fourth angel poured out his bowl on the sun, and the
sun was given power to scorch people with fire. ⁹They were
seared by the intense heat and they cursed the name of God,
who had control over these plagues, but they refused to repent
and glorify him.

The first bowl strikes the land and affects the emperor
worshipers (16:2). The second bowl turns the sea into blood
and the third does the same to the inland waters. Domitian
and his followers had made a blood bath of God's servants,
and now they were going to swim in their own! In 16:5, the
angel affirmed the rightness of God bringing about such a
severe judgment. The altar in 16:7 added its own approval.
The souls under the altar of sacrifice in 6:9-11 and the saints
whose prayers were offered at the altar of incense (8:3-5) are
thrilled to see justice done and their cause vindicated.

The fourth bowl (16:8-9) reveals the strong tendency of
sinful man to not only question the actions of God, but to
blame him for their problems. They pay no attention to him
and his desires for their lives when things are going well, but
when things are not going well they curse him. *Amazing*! Such
darkness of the soul is predictable when man offers no grati-
tude to his Maker. Paul described this progression into darkness with these words in Romans 1:21: "For although they
knew God, they neither glorified him as God nor gave thanks
to him, but their thinking became futile and their foolish hearts
were darkened."

All of us have to deal with the problem of human suffering. When we face the harsh realities of life, we come out on
one side of the coin or the other. One side blames God and
the other holds on to him, trusting that he is all-knowing, all-
loving and all-powerful. Faith will always be the issue while
we live on this earth. Whether we are standing at the grave of
a martyr in the first century or at the grave of a stillborn baby
in the twentieth, our broken hearts will cry out for light. The
Bible believer will decide to live with his incomplete

picture of the "whys" involved, pour out his anguish to the Father who still cares deeply, and await the final answers in the life to come.[1]

The Throne of the Beast Destroyed by the Last Three Bowls (16:10-21)

> [10]*The fifth angel poured out his bowl on the throne of the beast, and his kingdom was plunged into darkness. Men gnawed their tongues in agony* [11]*and cursed the God of heaven because of their pains and their sores, but they refused to repent of what they had done.*
>
> [12]*The sixth angel poured out his bowl on the great river Euphrates, and its water was dried up to prepare the way for the kings from the East.* [13]*Then I saw three evil spirits that looked like frogs; they came out of the mouth of the dragon, out of the mouth of the beast and out of the mouth of the false prophet.* [14]*They are spirits of demons performing miraculous signs, and they go out to the kings of the whole world, to gather them for the battle on the great day of God Almighty.*
>
> [15]*"Behold, I come like a thief! Blessed is he who stays awake and keeps his clothes with him, so that he may not go naked and be shamefully exposed."*
>
> [16]*Then they gathered the kings together to the place that in Hebrew is called Armageddon.*
>
> [17]*The seventh angel poured out his bowl into the air, and out of the temple came a loud voice from the throne, saying, "It is done!"* [18]*Then there came flashes of lightning, rumblings, peals of thunder and a severe earthquake. No earthquake like it has ever occurred since man has been on earth, so tremendous was the quake.* [19]*The great city split into three parts, and the cities of the nations collapsed. God remembered Babylon the Great and gave her the cup filled with the wine of the fury of his wrath.* [20]*Every island fled away and the mountains could not be found.* [21]*From the sky huge hailstones of about a hundred pounds each fell upon men. And they cursed God on account of the plague of hail, because the plague was so terrible.*

In the remainder of the bowls, the kingdom of the beast (the sea beast, political Rome) will be destroyed. As the fifth bowl is emptied, this kingdom is plunged into darkness. But even facing the intensified punishment, its subjects continue to curse God. With their last breath, they seem determined to curse him. Can you imagine what men in rebellion against their Judge are going to feel when they cross the threshold of death and meet him?

The sixth bowl is poured out on the Euphrates river (16:12), drying it up in order to permit invasion. This symbolism may trace back to Jeremiah's prophecy (50:38) that ancient Babylon's fall would be connected with her waters drying up. Almost certainly the very real threat of the Parthians from the east invading Rome was in view.

Three frogs (16:13) come out of the mouth of the dragon (Satan) and his allies (the sea beast of 13:1 and the false prophet—the land beast of 13:11). Frogs were unclean animals under the Mosaic Law (Leviticus 11:10), and they are not particularly appealing no matter what law you are under! In the vision they are demonic spirits, representing evil propaganda to deceive other nations into helping Rome against the forces of righteousness. Evil loves the comfort of large numbers, reasoning that "surely everyone can't be wrong." Romans 1 closes with a recognition of this principle:

> *Although they know God's righteous decree that those who do such things deserve death, they not only continue to do these very things but also approve of those who practice them. (Romans 1:32)*

But there is no safety in numbers. Again, we could ask the people of Noah's day about this one!

Back in 12:15-16, the dragon emitted a river of lies in an attempt to engulf the woman (the church). In 13:5, the beast uttered proud words and blasphemies out of his mouth. Satan is the father of lies. He knows how to use all types of lies, from the subtle to the blatant. The power to deceive is, according to this text, miraculous in effect. The only available antidote for the threat is truth, for it alone can make us free (John 8:31-32).

Our need to be spiritually aware and awake is described in 16:15, keeping our clothes with us at all time. From passages like Matthew 22:1-14, we learn that being clothed properly is tantamount to being adequately prepared. Since Jesus comes as a thief, we have to live each day as if it might be our last—because it just might!

Now we come to the final bowl and the famous battle of Armageddon (16:16-21). Books about Armageddon fill the shelves of religious bookstores. They make claims which are absolutely incredible and about a million miles distant from everything that Revelation is really all about. In front of me as I write is a catalogue from a major religious book distributor in which many books are pictured and described. A very representative title from the pamphlet is *Armageddon, Oil and the Middle East Crisis*, written by a well-respected scholar in the religious world, John Walvoord. Its description reads:

> Right now the stage is set in the Middle East for the final drama leading to Armageddon and Jesus' Second Coming. In this up-to-date book, he explains how Biblical prophecies are fulfilled in such recent events as the formation of the European Economic Community, the end of the Cold War, the Arab/Israeli conflict, and the occupation of Kuwait.[2]

Another book entitled *The Rise of Babylon* has a description that is slightly more sensational.

> In September 1987, Saddam Hussein invited Dyer [the author of the described book] and other foreigners to Iraq for a cultural festival. Included in that tour was a visit to the ancient city of Babylon, now being magnificently restored and rebuilt. Is Biblical prophecy about the last days being fulfilled? Using new photos, Dyer shows how Iraq's rise to power parallels the rise of ancient Babylon, and how Hussein is actually modeling himself after Nebuchadnezzar.[3]

If we have never heard the alternatives, we can be carried away with such sensational headlines and bylines. I can remember believing that all of it was true. The problem with such approaches is that books like these have been written for many years with very different applications. The key figures in speculative writings a half century ago were Stalin and Hitler. Later it was Khrushchev or some other Russian leader. Just about every American president has been "found" in the prophecies of Revelation, as have all of the key wars that have affected our country. No matter how many predictions have fallen by the wayside, another is brought forward to take its place. But whatever may be said of Armageddon in Revelation 16, it simply cannot be wrenched from its moorings and forced to mean anything and everything the speculators claim!

Well, what *does* it mean? Good question, and the answer is not complicated. The word means "Mount of Megiddo," which is a famous battleground in Israelite history. Decisive battles were fought there by famous people. Gideon and his three hundred men defeated the Midianites at Megiddo. Deborah and Barak overcame the Canaanite forces of King Jabin here. King Saul was defeated by the Philistines at Megiddo. It was here that Ahaziah died at the hands of Jehu, and also here that the Egyptian King Pharaoh-Necho killed Josiah. To those familiar with Jewish history, all of the figures and battles were larger-than-life. Therefore, as a famous battlefield it was a perfect *symbol* for the decisive battle between God's forces and Satan's in the showdown between Rome and righteousness. It is, like the dozens of other symbols in Revelation, just that—a symbol.

This final bowl is poured out into the air, because the devil is the prince of the powers of the air (Ephesians 2:2). The certainty of Rome's fall ("it is done") is described in 16:12. Since God is timeless (the great "I AM"—Exodus 3:14), all that *will be* is already in his mind. He resides in what we humans call "past, present and future" at the same time, which is one reason why we should trust him completely. He sees the end from the beginning and can easily fit all the parts together so that everything will work together for good (Romans 8:28). It is a guarantee and cannot fail!

The great earthquake divided the city into three parts (16:19), perhaps in answer to the three Satanic agents of false propaganda mentioned earlier in the chapter (16:13). In any event, the destruction is complete, brought about by the "mother of all earthquakes" (to borrow a middle-east warlord's phrase!). We should note here that the description of this earthquake makes use of a figure of speech called "hyperbole," an exaggeration to emphasize a point. Unless we understand this device, we will have difficulty not taking this description as a depiction of the end of the world. In predicting the destruction of Jerusalem which took place in 70 AD, Jesus made a similar statement during his ministry on earth: "For then there will be great distress, unequaled from the beginning of the world until now—and never to be equaled again" (Matthew 24:21).[4] In both cases, a strong emphasis is being made to show the utter devastation that was fast approaching. The bowls had accomplished what they were designed to do, namely deliver the deathblow to the persecuting empire of the beast and false prophet.

?   What kind of lies from Satan cause you the most problems? How well do you think you understand how Satan works? Describe how he works in your life. Have you read *The Lion Never Sleeps* by Mike Taliaferro?[5] If not, do it soon!

13

▼

His Terrible Swift Sword
REVELATION 17, 18 AND 19

In Revelation 5, Jesus was depicted as the lamb and the lion. Nowhere will his lionlike characteristics be more readily apparent than in the passage we are about to consider. He is the fierce warrior who attacks the enemies of his people, reducing them to a pile of decaying corpses, the main course for a feast of vultures!

Babylon's fall has been announced (16:19). Now we have a thorough description of this fall, and the worldliness of Rome is exposed and condemned. In one sense, it seems unusual that the pouring out of the bowls of God's final wrath would be followed by an introduction of the third ally of Satan (the prostitute). However, in another sense, it is very logical. Babylon, otherwise identified as "the prostitute," signifies the materialistic aspect of Rome. More than either the political or religious aspects, the worldliness offered by Rome lay closest to the heart of its subjects. Intellectual philosophy was one thing; life-style was quite another. To those without deep spiritual convictions, nothing seems more important than the freedom to be self-indulgent.

The Prostitute Riding a Scarlet Beast (17:1-18)

Obviously, God wanted to deeply impress the readers with his absolute disgust of materialism. He hated both the corrupt political and religious aspects of Rome, to be sure, but even we Bible-believers underestimate his hatred of materialistic worldliness. Consider the words of Jesus:

> *"No servant can serve two masters. Either he will hate the one and love the other, or he will be devoted to the one and despise the other. You cannot serve both God and Money."*
> *The Pharisees, who loved money, heard all this and were sneering at Jesus. He said to them, "You are the ones who*

justify yourselves in the eyes of men, but God knows your hearts. What is highly valued among men is detestable in God's sight." (Luke 16:13-15)

By the time God is finished with the detailed descriptions in Revelation 17 and 18, we can almost picture him rubbing his hands together and saying, "Yes! Amen!" at the demise of Babylon. And we should picture him asking us to really examine just how important life-style and personal financial comfort are to us. The sobering truth for most of us is that our purse strings are much too closely connected to our heartstrings.

The Prostitute Introduced (17:1-6)

[17:1]One of the seven angels who had the seven bowls came and said to me, "Come, I will show you the punishment of the great prostitute, who sits on many waters. [2]With her the kings of the earth committed adultery and the inhabitants of the earth were intoxicated with the wine of her adulteries."

[3]Then the angel carried me away in the Spirit into a desert. There I saw a woman sitting on a scarlet beast that was covered with blasphemous names and had seven heads and ten horns. [4]The woman was dressed in purple and scarlet, and was glittering with gold, precious stones and pearls. She held a golden cup in her hand, filled with abominable things and the filth of her adulteries. [5]This title was written on her forehead:

MYSTERY
BABYLON THE GREAT
THE MOTHER OF PROSTITUTES
AND OF THE ABOMINATIONS OF THE EARTH.

[6]I saw that the woman was drunk with the blood of the saints, the blood of those who bore testimony to Jesus.
When I saw her, I was greatly astonished.

The first verse makes it clear that the introduction of the prostitute is an elaboration of the fall of Babylon announced in 16:19. An angel who had poured out one of the bowls of wrath is the one showing John the punishment of the prostitute. This woman is sitting upon many waters, which suggests ancient Babylon on the Euphrates River (see Jeremiah 51:12-13). The application is to Rome sitting (ruling) over many peoples (17:15). She committed immorality with kings of earth—spiritual immorality, worldliness in the extreme. 1 John 2:15-17 (NASB) gives us an explicit definition of the love of the world in these words:

> *Do not love the world, nor the things in the world. If anyone loves the world, the love of the Father is not in him. For all that is in the world, the lust of the flesh and the lust of the eyes and the boastful pride of life, is not from the Father, but is from the world. And the world is passing away, and also its lusts; but the one who does the will of God abides forever.*

The prostitute rode on the back of the beast (17:3) first introduced in 13:1 (compare the two descriptions). Political Rome made materialistic Rome possible. The beast is scarlet colored, for his sins were indeed as scarlet (Isaiah 1:18).

The golden cup full of abominable things (17:4) shows how attractive worldliness looks but how it yields despicable results. A good commentary on this figure is Jeremiah 51:7: "Babylon was a gold cup in the LORD's hand; she made the whole earth drunk. The nations drank her wine; therefore they have now gone mad."

In our present passage (17:6), the woman is drunk. She is like a *vampire*, craving the blood of the saints! The worldly heart hates the spiritual heart, and under the right circumstances the amount of hatred will be revealed.

The Mystery of the Woman and Beast Explained (17:7-18)

> [7]*Then the angel said to me: "Why are you astonished? I will explain to you the mystery of the woman and of the beast she rides, which has the seven heads and ten horns.* [8]*The beast, which you saw, once was, now is not, and will come up out of the Abyss and go to his destruction. The inhabitants of the earth whose names have not been written in the book of life from the creation of the world will be astonished when they see the beast, because he once was, now is not, and yet will come.*
>
> [9]*"This calls for a mind with wisdom. The seven heads are seven hills on which the woman sits.* [10]*They are also seven kings. Five have fallen, one is, the other has not yet come; but when he does come, he must remain for a little while.* [11]*The beast who once was, and now is not, is an eighth king. He belongs to the seven and is going to his destruction.*

> [12]*"The ten horns you saw are ten kings who have not yet received a kingdom, but who for one hour will receive authority as kings along with the beast.* [13]*They have one purpose and will give their power and authority to the beast.* [14]*They will make war against the Lamb, but the Lamb will overcome them because he is Lord of lords and King of kings—and with him will be his called, chosen and faithful followers."*
>
> [15]*Then the angel said to me, "The waters you saw, where the prostitute sits, are peoples, multitudes, nations and languages.* [16]*The beast and the ten horns you saw will hate the prostitute. They will bring her to ruin and leave her naked; they will eat her flesh and burn her with fire.* [17]*For God has put it into their hearts to accomplish his purpose by agreeing to give the beast their power to rule, until God's words are fulfilled.* [18]*The woman you saw is the great city that rules over the kings of the earth."*

The angel's question, "Why are you astonished?" is a good one for us. We should not be *perplexed* at the figures in Revelation. God expects us to understand them. It is true that the book is not easy to comprehend without help in understanding apocalyptic language, but once we get the gist of such language, most passages become reasonably clear. However, the one we are about to discuss is one of the more difficult ones in the book. As with all symbols, I am making my best attempt to interpret them in light of my study. I am not listing all the possibilities or the interpretations given by others. There may be a place for such an approach, but the length of this exposition prohibits it. With these things in mind, let's delve into the interpretation of the series of kings which make up the beast.

The beast of 17:8 seems to reflect the Nero Redivivus Myth (seen back in 13:3). The beast who "once was and is not" would refer to Nero, who was, at the time of writing, deceased. The statement "will come out of the Abyss" (17:8) would refer to Domitian who came in the spirit and power of Nero, the first major persecutor of Christians. The difficulty is that we have been assuming the book described the persecution under Domitian which was already occurring by 95 AD. If the book was written then, as most conservative scholars believe, how could Domitian be the one whom "yet will come"? (17:8). As we move into the next section of the passage, hopefully it will become clearer.

The seven heads of the beast are described as seven kings (17:10). Five of them have fallen, one is, one will come for a brief time, and finally an eighth king comes. Normally in Revelation, the number "seven" is used only symbolically. However, because of the specifics given, we knew that the seven churches described in Revelation 2 and 3 were literal. (Of course, in that case symbolism is also indicated because the complete church of Asia was represented, and perhaps the universal church.) In our present passage, enough specifics are given to conclude that we are being given a progression of actual kings. If this is true, we know that the eighth emperor was Domitian because of what was said in 17:8. Backtracking from there, we can come up with this probable list:

1. Augustus	5. Nero
2. Tiberius	6. Vespasian
3. Caligula	7. Titus
4. Claudius	8. Domitian

The listing begins with Augustus instead of Julius Caesar, who is often called the first emperor. However, Augustus was the first to rule the empire with its government constitutionally established. The list also omits three kings (Galba, Otho, and Vitellius) who reigned very briefly after Nero, but were not recognized as emperors in the provinces. Otherwise, the listing is in the order of succession as they occurred historically. Titus did reign only for a "brief time" (79-81 AD), which fits into the series as described. If we accept the listing as indicating literal kings, then John received his visions during the reign of Vespasian (69-79 AD). The revelation would have been published in 95 AD during Domitian's reign after John left the island of Patmos, which would account for the popular tradition regarding the date of the book.

As intriguing as all such "figuring" may be, what real difference does it make? Probably not too much. The beast was clearly the Roman empire regardless of the specific emperor on the throne. And it was a beast doomed to destruction (17:8, 11). This is the main point, although John left us with the possibility of trying to determine the order of the kings.

The ten kings of 17:12 are simply mentioned as a group, which makes it very probable that they are merely symbolic of future emperors who would carry on the ungodly mission of the persecuting political system. However, the Lord of lords and the King of kings would bring them to the same bitter end as Domitian.

The many waters on which the prostitutes sat (17:15) are defined here as "peoples, multitudes, nations and languages," showing the diverse nature of the sprawling empire. The point will be reached, according to 17:16, when the political aspect of Rome would grow to hate the prostitute. These rulers turned against her worldly influence because sin had done its job too well. We have previously pictured the internal decay which played such a large part in the downfall of Rome. The Roman Senate encouraged moral and ethical laxity, just as our political system has today, but the resultant degradation even shocked them. Satan knows how to take sin further than nearly anyone anticipates, and certainly further than nearly anyone enjoys. Sin feeds on itself and multiplies into a monster. Are we not seeing the proof before our very eyes in our own societies today?

? How important are material possessions to you? How important is comfort and ease of life-style? Do you have the same attitude toward these things as God does? How willing would you be to sacrifice your present life-style if doing so would further the spread of the kingdom? How sensitive are you to appeals for increased contributions in the church? Do you need help with your heart in these matters? Will you ask for it?

The Fall of Babylon the Great (18:1-24)

Revelation 18 is what might be called a "funeral dirge." As the fall of the city (depicting Rome) is announced and described, the symbols are borrowed from the OT prophets. Particularly, the ones used in portraying the downfall of literal Babylon (Isaiah 13:20-22, Jeremiah 50:39, 51:37), Nineveh (Zephaniah 2:13-15) and Tyre (Ezekiel 26-28). The symbolism of 18:22-24, showing the cessation of entertainment life, business life and home life is taken from Jeremiah 16:9, 25:10, and Ezekiel 26:13. To receive the strongest impact from this lament, we need only to read it straight through. Only a few words of explanation are really necessary.

> [18:1]*After this I saw another angel coming down from heaven. He had great authority, and the earth was illuminated by his splendor.* [2]*With a mighty voice he shouted:*

"Fallen! Fallen is Babylon the Great!
  She has become a home for demons
and a haunt for every evil spirit,
  a haunt for every unclean and detestable bird.
³For all the nations have drunk
  the maddening wine of her adulteries.
The kings of the earth committed adultery with her,
  and the merchants of the earth grew rich from her
  excessive luxuries."

18:3 gives us a vivid picture of how God equates luxurious living with spiritual adultery. But materialism is not confined to possessing—it includes a *desire* to possess. James 4:4 described such a desire in these words: "You adulterous people, don't you know that friendship with the world is hatred toward God? Anyone who chooses to be a friend of the world becomes an enemy of God." The NASB uses the word "wishes" instead of "chooses," which gets to the heart of the issue, namely our desires.

Since all of us struggle with the desire for possessions, what is the cure? We must replace this desire with a far better desire—the desire to carry out the Great Commission in our generation. This motivation should make us increasingly willing to sacrifice our personal finances for the Cause of world evangelism. For most of us, giving a tithe is really not sacrifice. Remember that God evaluates our giving in terms of what we have left after giving, not by the amount actually given (Luke 21:1-4).

The early church understood the concept of stewardship well (Acts 2:44-45, 32-36). They viewed all possessions as first belonging to God and secondly to their brothers and sisters in Christ. The sacrifices were made for the same mission goal we profess today. The new converts from other cities and nations needed support in order to be trained and sent back to their home areas. The nature of the mission has not substantially changed. Have our hearts?

⁴Then I heard another voice from heaven say:

"Come out of her, my people,
  so that you will not share in her sins,
  so that you will not receive any of her plagues;
⁵for her sins are piled up to heaven,
  and God has remembered her crimes.

> *⁶Give back to her as she has given;*
> *pay her back double for what she has done.*
> *Mix her a double portion from her own cup.*
> *⁷Give her as much torture and grief*
> *as the glory and luxury she gave herself.*
> *In her heart she boasts,*
> *'I sit as queen; I am not a widow,*
> *and I will never mourn.'*
> *⁸Therefore in one day her plagues will overtake her:*
> *death, mourning and famine.*
> *She will be consumed by fire,*
> *for mighty is the Lord God who judges her."*

As 18:4 makes clear, worldliness is a broad topic. It is more than materialism, though it includes the love of things. Without doubt, it is naturally attractive even to the strongest of disciples. Therefore, we must be aware of the progression of worldliness in our lives and come out of it. It begins with a desire to be *friends* with the world (James 4:4), moves to having some *corruption* by the world, (James 1:27), then to *conformity* with the world (Romans 12:2) and ends with being *condemned* with the world (1 Corinthians 11:32).

The law of harvest is always true—we reap what we sow. This is the message of 18:6-7. As in the case with farming, at times it is difficult to determine what is happening with the seeds being planted. But come up they will, in direct proportion to what and how they have been planted.

> *⁹"When the kings of the earth who committed adultery with her and shared her luxury see the smoke of her burning, they will weep and mourn over her. ¹⁰Terrified at her torment, they will stand far off and cry:*
>
> *"'Woe! Woe, O great city,*
> *O Babylon, city of power!*
> *In one hour your doom has come!'*
>
> *¹¹"The merchants of the earth will weep and mourn over her because no one buys their cargoes any more— ¹²cargoes of gold, silver, precious stones and pearls; fine linen, purple, silk and scarlet cloth; every sort of citron wood, and articles of every kind made of ivory, costly wood, bronze, iron and marble; ¹³cargoes of cinnamon and spice, of incense, myrrh*

and frankincense, of wine and olive oil, of fine flour and wheat; cattle and sheep; horses and carriages; and bodies and souls of men.

14"They will say, 'The fruit you longed for is gone from you. All your riches and splendor have vanished, never to be recovered.' 15The merchants who sold these things and gained their wealth from her will stand far off, terrified at her torment. They will weep and mourn 16and cry out:

> *"'Woe! Woe, O great city,*
> *dressed in fine linen, purple and scarlet,*
> *and glittering with gold, precious stones and pearls!*
> *17In one hour such great wealth has been brought to ruin!'*

"Every sea captain, and all who travel by ship, the sailors, and all who earn their living from the sea, will stand far off. 18When they see the smoke of her burning, they will exclaim, 'Was there ever a city like this great city?' 19They will throw dust on their heads, and with weeping and mourning cry out:

> *"'Woe! Woe, O great city,*
> *where all who had ships on the sea*
> *became rich through her wealth!*
> *In one hour she has been brought to ruin!*
> *20Rejoice over her, O heaven!*
> *Rejoice, saints and apostles and prophets!*
> *God has judged her for the way she treated you.'"*

21Then a mighty angel picked up a boulder the size of a large millstone and threw it into the sea, and said:

> *"With such violence*
> *the great city of Babylon will be thrown down,*
> *never to be found again.*
> *22The music of harpists and musicians,*
> *flute players and trumpeters,*
> *will never be heard in you again.*
> *No workman of any trade*
> *will ever be found in you again.*
> *The sound of a millstone*
> *will never be heard in you again.*
> *23The light of a lamp*
> *will never shine in you again.*
> *The voice of bridegroom and bride*
> *will never be heard in you again.*

> *Your merchants were the world's great men.*
>   *By your magic spell all the nations were led astray.*
> [24]*In her was found the blood of prophets and of the saints,*
>   *and of all who have been killed on the earth."*

The world will be judged by its response to righteousness and righteous people (18:20). The desire for personal vengeance on the part of the righteous is unneeded, for nothing escapes the attention and justice of God. However, prayers for the vindication of God's cause are appropriate and will be answered (6:9-10, 8:3-5). The blood of the children of God will be avenged either in this life or in the next, and justice will prevail. This reckoning is as sure as the promises of God.

The Beast and the False Prophet Fall

The Hallelujah Chorus! (19:1-10)

> [19:1]*After this I heard what sounded like the roar of a great multitude in heaven shouting:*
>
> > *"Hallelujah!*
> > *Salvation and glory and power belong to our God,*
> >   [2]*for true and just are his judgments.*
> > *He has condemned the great prostitute*
> >   *who corrupted the earth by her adulteries.*
> > *He has avenged on her the blood of his servants."*
>
> [3]*And again they shouted:*
>
> > *"Hallelujah!*
> > *The smoke from her goes up for ever and ever."*
>
> [4]*The twenty-four elders and the four living creatures fell down and worshiped God, who was seated on the throne. And they cried:*
>
> > *"Amen, Hallelujah!"*
>
> [5]*Then a voice came from the throne, saying:*
>
> > *"Praise our God,*
> >   *all you his servants,*
> > *you who fear him,*
> >   *both small and great!"*

⁶Then I heard what sounded like a great multitude, like the roar of rushing waters and like loud peals of thunder, shouting:

"Hallelujah!
For our Lord God Almighty reigns.
⁷Let us rejoice and be glad
and give him glory!
For the wedding of the Lamb has come,
and his bride has made herself ready.

⁸Fine linen, bright and clean,
was given her to wear."

(Fine linen stands for the righteous acts of the saints.)

⁹Then the angel said to me, "Write: 'Blessed are those who are invited to the wedding supper of the Lamb!' " And he added, "These are the true words of God."
¹⁰At this I fell at his feet to worship him. But he said to me, "Do not do it! I am a fellow servant with you and with your brothers who hold to the testimony of Jesus. Worship God! For the testimony of Jesus is the spirit of prophecy."

In stark contrast to the lamenting wails with which the previous chapter ended, we open Revelation 19 to the sound of loud rejoicing. We are familiar with the popular *Hallelujah Chorus* by Handel, but this section introduces the real hallelujah chorus! The word "hallelujah" simply means "praise God." It is found only here (19:1, 3, 4, 6) in the Scriptures (NIV). This scarcity of usage may seem odd to those who have a background in Pentecostal churches and are used to lots of "hallelujahs." But this passage does mark the word as a special one, using it to honor God for bringing about the destruction of his enemies as he vindicates the cause of his saints.

Revelation 19 contains two great suppers: the wedding supper for the saints (19:7-9), and the vulture's dinner (19:17-18). The wedding of the Lamb marks the ultimate relationship we will have with the Lord in eternity. Christians now are in one sense engaged to Christ (2 Corinthians 11:2), married in another sense (Romans 7:4), but the marriage supper is still in the future (consider also Ephesians 5:22-32). Our presence with him will mark the official consummation of our marriage.

John says that "fine linen" (the righteous acts of the saints) was given to the bride to wear (19:8)—a reminder that the righteousness of the church is a gift from God. The church will indeed do righteous things, but those are the result of God's grace and not some righteousness of her own (Philippians 3:9, Ephesians 2:8-10).

In 19:10, John is overcome by the vision to the point that he falls down to worship the angel showing him the visions. He does the same thing again in 22:8-9, with the same results. The angel makes it clear that only God is to be worshiped, and he is not God. Jesus says in Matthew 4:10, "Away from me, Satan! For it is written: 'Worship the Lord your God, and serve him only.'" We also know that no man can be worshiped (Acts 10:25-26, 14:11-18). Since Jesus was worshiped both by men (Matthew 8:2, 9:18, 14:33, 15:25, John 20:28) and by angels (Hebrews 1:6, Revelation 5), the only possible conclusion is that he is God and not a created or secondary being (Jehovah Witness doctrine notwithstanding).

Jesus on a White Horse (19:11-16)

>[11]I saw heaven standing open and there before me was a white horse, whose rider is called Faithful and True. With justice he judges and makes war. [12]His eyes are like blazing fire, and on his head are many crowns. He has a name written on him that no one knows but he himself. [13]He is dressed in a robe dipped in blood, and his name is the Word of God. [14]The armies of heaven were following him, riding on white horses and dressed in fine linen, white and clean. [15]Out of his mouth comes a sharp sword with which to strike down the nations. "He will rule them with an iron scepter." He treads the winepress of the fury of the wrath of God Almighty. [16]On his robe and on his thigh he has this name written:
>
>KING OF KINGS AND LORD OF LORDS.

Jesus, the Word of God, enters the drama riding on a white horse (19:11). Babylon has fallen, and now the other two allies of Satan are about to meet their final end. The descriptions of Jesus are identical or very similar to others scattered throughout the book. He has a name written on him that no one can really know (19:12). Only Jesus himself can understand his personality and deity, although those with spiritual hearts can know him to the extent that he has revealed himself and to the extent that mortals are able to understand. His robe is dipped blood because he is engaged in a war with the spiritual forces of evil. As he said in Matthew 10:34, "Do not suppose that I have come to bring peace to the earth. I did not come to bring peace, but a sword." That sword, of course, is the sword of the Spirit, the Word of God (Ephesians 6:17).

In 19:13, Jesus is called the Word of God, which is reminiscent of his description in John 1:1-3 as the eternal *Logos* (Word). To the Hebrew mind, *logos* was the written word of God. To the Greek mind, *logos* was wisdom. For the Jews, he lived and taught the message which became the New Testament, God's final written revelation. For the Greeks, he was God's final revelation of wisdom, for he was the One "in whom are hidden all the treasures of wisdom and knowledge" (Colossians 2:3). He is the "KING OF KINGS AND THE LORD OF LORDS." No matter what the puny human emperors may say of themselves or hear from others, they had a master who was destined to exercise his authority over them. If we fear him, we need fear no man. Isaiah put it this way:

> "...*do not fear what they fear,*
>   *and do not dread it.*
> *The LORD Almighty is the one you are to regard as holy,*
>   *he is the one you are to fear,*
>   *he is the one you are to dread,*
> *and he will be a sanctuary." (Isaiah 8:12-14)*

Doom of the Beast and False Prophet (19:17-21)

[17]And I saw an angel standing in the sun, who cried in a loud voice to all the birds flying in midair, "Come, gather together for the great supper of God, [18]so that you may eat the flesh of kings, generals, and mighty men, of horses and their riders, and the flesh of all people, free and slave, small and great."

[19]Then I saw the beast and the kings of the earth and their armies gathered together to make war against the rider on the horse and his army. [20]But the beast was captured, and with him the false prophet who had performed the miraculous signs on his behalf. With these signs he had deluded those who had received the mark of the beast and worshiped his image. The

*two of them were thrown alive into the fiery lake of burning
sulfur. [21]The rest of them were killed with the sword that came
out of the mouth of the rider on the horse, and all the birds
gorged themselves on their flesh.*

God's second supper is introduced, which will be vultures
feasting on the flesh of his enemies. All of them are pictured
as joining in the battle against the Christ, but he has "loosed
the faithful lightning of his terrible swift sword," and they are
destroyed (19:21). The beast and false prophet are captured
alive in the vision and cast into hell. The allies of Satan are
decimated at last, leaving only Satan to meet his doom, which
Revelation 20 describes. The scene ends with the birds gorg-
ing themselves on God's fallen enemies—an ignoble end to
those who once were exalted by men to the position reserved
for God alone. However, as has become obvious, God will
brook no rivals!

? How would you define "Christlikeness"? Does the picture of Christ in this chapter
harmonize with your definition? Explain. Which areas of your life do you need to
change in order to become more like him? Can we be like Jesus without causing
negative reactions against us? How do you feel about such reactions?

14
▼

Satan Bound, Loosed, Then Destroyed
REVELATION 20

Finally, we reach the passage which speaks of the famous thousand-year reign. Now we can find out just what all of this mysterious symbolism means! Honestly, if a person had never heard all of the modern speculative theories, this passage would not provoke any more notice than any other passage in the book. In context, it fits right into the final defeat of God's enemies, and the last to be destroyed is Satan. He is introduced, bound, loosed and defeated. No huge mystery here. Had it not been for the mention of a thousand-year reign here, perhaps much of the modern theory would never have developed. Without question, Revelation 20 provides the key foundation upon which these millennial theories are based. But all we need to do is follow the same line of reasoning we have followed up until now. If we merely keep in mind the historical background of the book, the nature of apocalyptic writing and its purpose here of comforting persecuted Christians at the end of the first century, we cannot go far afield.

In approaching this or other difficult passages, several fundamental rules of interpretation must be kept in mind:

- Truth does not contradict itself. If two verses seem to contradict each other, there is either misunderstanding of one of the verses or possibly both of them.
- Doctrine cannot be based on difficult passages without due consideration of less difficult passages on the same subject. To establish a theory on symbolic passages forces us to completely ignore literal passages which contradict it and also to apply figurative interpretation to obviously literal Scriptures.

- We do not have to know exactly what a difficult passage means in order to know what it *does not* mean. For example, a person could be unsure of the exact inter-pretation of 1 Corinthians 15:29, but at the same time be absolutely sure that it does not teach proxy baptism for the physically dead. Too many plain passages render that explanation impossible. In a similar way, one could be somewhat uncertain of the precise meaning of some of the symbolism in Revelation, while rejecting the doctrine of premillennialism itself.

Before proceeding to the exposition of Revelation 20, it will prove helpful to mention a few issues relating to the confusion caused by the spread of the premillennial doctrine. In the sim-plest terms the premillenial view says that Jesus will return to earth, establish a physical kingdom with its headquarters in Jerusalem and will reign there for a literal thousand years. As noted in Chapter 1, associated doctrines are often the rapture of the righteous to heaven seven years prior to Christ's return; the appearance of a personal Antichrist; a Great Tribulation just prior to Christ's return; and a literal battle of Armegeddon. Even a brief look at Revelation 20:1-10 raises at least two fundamental problems for the premillennial advocates.

One, the text does not, in fact, mention a number of things people assume are being taught. The second coming of Christ is not mentioned—Christ is not even mentioned as being *on earth*. No mention is specifically made of *anyone* reigning on earth. A bodily resurrection is not mentioned; and finally, no one living in modern times is mentioned in connection with this thousand-year reign. The *persecuted* of the early church are the ones who sit on thrones and reign with Christ. Now, how can this passage mention *none* of these things and yet teach *all* of them?

Two, this passage is full of figurative symbolic language. If we insist on making the thousand years literal, why are not the key to the abyss, the great chain, the beast, etc. also literal?

Satan Is Bound (20:1-3)

> *20:1And I saw an angel coming down out of heaven, having the key to the Abyss and holding in his hand a great chain.*

*²He seized the dragon, that ancient serpent, who is the devil,
or Satan, and bound him for a thousand years. ³He threw him
into the Abyss, and locked and sealed it over him, to keep him
from deceiving the nations anymore until the thousand years
were ended. After that, he must be set free for a short time.*

The point of these first several verses is that Satan had to
be bound in order to stop his horrifying actions against the
first century disciples of the Lamb. When his three allies met
their demise, he was then limited in some way, to some de-
gree. In this dramatic vision, the angel comes down on a mission from God with a key to the Abyss. The Abyss, as we have
noted earlier, is the residing place of the demonic forces. The
key to it denotes the angel's authority to access this place and
bind up Satan with the chain he brought for that purpose.
Just like Peter had the keys of the kingdom, allowing him to
open it to the Jews and later the Gentiles, the angel had the
keys to allow him entrance into the devil's lair.

In what way was Satan bound? Not entirely, for he remained
the roaring lion of which Peter spoke (1 Peter 5:8).[1] Being bound
meant that he was *limited* in some way. He became like a
chained dog, who was still quite ferocious within the length
of the chain, but limited in how far he could reach. Of course,
Satan's limitations were all due to the work of Christ (Matthew 12:29, Luke 10:17-18). He was limited in some manner
for a thousand years, signifying a long period of time. As noted
in Chapter 1 of this book, 1,000, a multiple of ten (10 × 10 ×
10), is the number of ultimate completeness. It is not to be
taken literally any more than the other numbers in Revelation. (The only exceptions to a symbolic interpretation we have
seen thus far were the seven churches and possibly the seven
kings in Revelation 17, because of the specifics involved which
made such treatment appropriate.)

Satan was locked and sealed in the Abyss and will not be
released until the thousand years are over. In a similar passage,
Jude had this to say about the treatment of Satan's angels:

*And the angels who did not keep their positions of authority
but abandoned their own home—these he has kept in darkness, bound with everlasting chains for judgment on the great
Day. (Jude 1:6)*

It should be obvious that these forces of Satan are loose in some ways, working for Satan against all that is holy, but in some way they too are bound. The point is that the binding of Satan does not mean that he was totally incapacitated.

Our text informs us that the purpose of his limitation was to keep him from further deceiving the nations. How had he deceived them during the period of the persecution? For one thing, he had deceived them into a worldwide persecution of Christians. For another thing, he had duped them into emperor worship. Both of these deceptions depended upon the world being unified in a remarkable way under the banner of Rome. (Of course, it could be noted that he also deceived the nations into rejecting Christ. But that was nothing new and nothing which has changed in the years between then and now. This situation has always been a part of the broad way/narrow way scenario—Matthew 7:13-14.) Once the thousand years are over, Satan will persuade the nations to resume the same deception seen in the days of the persecuting Roman empire. After inserting Revelation 20:4-6 as a parenthetical explanation, the release of Satan is further described (20:7-10) which we will comment on more when we reach that passage.

Reigning with Christ (20:4-6)

> [4]I saw thrones on which were seated those who had been given authority to judge. And I saw the souls of those who had been beheaded because of their testimony for Jesus and because of the word of God. They had not worshiped the beast or his image and had not received his mark on their foreheads or their hands. They came to life and reigned with Christ a thousand years. [5](The rest of the dead did not come to life until the thousand years were ended.) This is the first resurrection. [6]Blessed and holy are those who have part in the first resurrection. The second death has no power over them, but they will be priests of God and of Christ and will reign with him for a thousand years.

Now we see those who are reigning on thrones along with the souls of those who lost their lives in the persecution. Whether dead or alive, the saints are now pictured as reigning in victory with Christ. The souls under the altar in 6:9 are now elevated to thrones—a symbolic way of showing the victory of their Cause. The scene reminds us of 11:11-12, where the two faithful witnesses who appeared to be dead were raised to life. Their apparently dead Cause was resurrected by the power of God. The symbols are similar in both passages and are the same in the lesson being conveyed: God's martyrs will not have given their lives in vain, because their movement will triumph over Satan. When he is bound for this long period of time (a thousand years), their Cause is brought back to life.

John calls this the "first resurrection" to distinguish it from the physical resurrection of the dead at the end of time. John's gospel also mentions both a spiritual type of resurrection and the physical resurrection in the same context (John 5:25 and 5:28-29).

The statement in 20:5, "the rest of the dead did not come to life," is a parenthetical statement showing that the non-Christian world, or particularly the persecutors, did not come to life during the thousand years. Their cause lies in defeat for a long time period (a thousand years symbolizes this period), but will briefly arise at some future date (20:7-10). Their cause of unrighteousness was defeated, and Satan was bound. They once had the upper hand, but had lost it to the Christian church. The ones who had seemed to be defeated were reigning with Christ, while the cause of the once victorious heathens was now lying dormant. The status of these two causes had switched.

Two key OT passages will help us to see the applications more clearly. The victory of God's cause is shown by a resurrection of the dead in Ezekiel 37. Read the passage carefully to see the similarity of the figures.

> *The hand of the L*ORD *was upon me, and he brought me out by the Spirit of the L*ORD *and set me in the middle of a valley; it was full of bones. He led me back and forth among them, and I saw a great many bones on the floor of the valley, bones that were very dry. He asked me, "Son of man, can these bones live?"*
>
> *I said, "O Sovereign L*ORD*, you alone know."*
>
> *Then he said to me, "Prophesy to these bones and say to them, 'Dry bones, hear the word of the L*ORD*! This is what the Sovereign L*ORD *says to these bones: I will make breath enter you, and you will come to life. I will attach tendons to you and make flesh come upon you and cover you with skin; I will put*

*breath in you, and you will come to life. Then you will know
that I am the LORD.' "*

*So I prophesied as I was commanded. And as I was proph-
esying, there was a noise, a rattling sound, and the bones
came together, bone to bone. I looked, and tendons and flesh
appeared on them and skin covered them, but there was no
breath in them.*

*Then he said to me, "Prophesy to the breath; prophesy,
son of man, and say to it, 'This is what the Sovereign LORD
says: Come from the four winds, O breath, and breathe into
these slain, that they may live.' " So I prophesied as he commanded me, and breath entered them; they came to life and
stood up on their feet—a vast army.*

*Then he said to me: "Son of man, these bones are the whole
house of Israel. They say, 'Our bones are dried up and our
hope is gone; we are cut off.'*

*Therefore prophesy and say to them: 'This is what the
Sovereign LORD says: O my people, I am going to open your
graves and bring you up from them; I will bring you back to
the land of Israel. Then you, my people, will know that I am
the LORD, when I open your graves and bring you up from
them. (Ezekiel 37:1-13)*

The prophet was not describing a literal resurrection from
the dead. He was describing the return of Israel to their home-
land from the lands to which they had been taken captive.
The people believed their cause to be lost forever, but God
had other plans. By the use of a vast horde of corpses being
raised, he showed them very vividly that their cause would
one day live and accomplish all that he had promised. Similarly, the cause of Jesus and his kingdom was going to live
and accomplish all of his promises.

A passage from Isaiah is used in a parallel manner to Revelation 20:5, describing a defeated cause that will not come to
life. Read it carefully to see their similarities:

> *O LORD, our God, other lords besides
>   you have ruled over us,
> but your name alone do we honor.
> They are now dead, they live no more;
>   those departed spirits do not rise.
> You punished them and brought them to ruin;
>   you wiped out all memory of them...*

But your dead will live;
their bodies will rise.
You who dwell in the dust,
wake up and shout for joy.
Your dew is like the dew of the morning;
the earth will give birth to her dead.
(Isaiah 26:13-14, 19)

The comparison of these OT passages with Revelation 20 shows the logic of seeing the resurrection figure as a symbolic one rather than a literal one. The background of the chapter included the defeat of Satan's allies in previous chapters, accounting for his limitations of influence over the nations. He was thus "bound." Unless and until he is able to create a similar situation among the nations at some future point, he will remain bound. However, our next section of verses tells us that he once again will have such a worldwide success. To those who love righteousness, this prospect is a terrifying one.

Satan Is Released (20:7-10)

[7]When the thousand years are over, Satan will be released from his prison [8]and will go out to deceive the nations in the four corners of the earth—Gog and Magog—to gather them for battle. In number they are like the sand on the seashore. [9]They marched across the breadth of the earth and surrounded the camp of God's people, the city he loves. But fire came down from heaven and devoured them. [10]And the devil, who deceived them, was thrown into the lake of burning sulfur, where the beast and the false prophet had been thrown. They will be tormented day and night for ever and ever.

According to 20:7-10, Satan will be loosed out of his prison when the thousand years are over. Since the thousand years describe the time of his being bound, the end of the this long time period would mark the removal of Satan's limitation. In comparison with the time he was bound (symbolic of a long period), the loosing would be for a "short time" (20:3). When he is released, he will deceive the nations once more. The type of deception will be the same as that which occurred in the Roman days. The deception of the nations (20:3) may indicate a worldwide persecution of Christians once more. And it may indicate that something akin to the worship of an empire will again commence. Again, the unity of the world would be presupposed in order to accomplish these ends.

"Gog and Magog" are mentioned (20:8) as representative of the nations deceived by Satan. These names come from the book of Ezekiel, especially chapters 38 and 39. In Ezekiel 38:2, Magog is the land over which the prince, Gog, rules. In Ezekiel 39:6, Magog seems also to be the name of a people. Suffice it to say that attempts to identify these names with modern nations will be no more accurate than other attempts to construe Revelation as a twentieth-century newspaper. The names are simply symbolic of evil nations as a whole, as Revelation 20:8 indicates plainly.

In this dramatic vision (20:7-10), these enemies of God surrounded the camp of the saints, his city and his church. At that point, fire out of heaven devours them. These figures come from Ezekiel 38:22 and 39:6, where they also simply describe the destruction of God's enemies. Because of the context, the fire in this present passage may refer to the fire associated with Christ's second coming. If so, 2 Thessalonians 1:7-8 is a good cross reference.

The section ends with the devil cast into hell, joining the beast and false prophet (19:20) and all the wicked (20:14-15, 21:8). Their destruction is certain and complete—day and night for ever and ever! The Bible does not answer every question about Satan's work, but it leaves absolutely no doubt as to his ultimate end.

Some pressing questions come to mind at this point. Is this release of Satan still in the future? It would seem to be, if the release of Satan is only for a short time which ends with the coming of Christ and the Judgment Day. When will the nations resume similar activities of persecution? If the earlier worldwide persecution began with a worldwide spread of the gospel, the same phenomenon will precede the upcoming torrent of persecution. (Surely many of us need no reminders of the amazing accomplishments in this direction taking place at this very moment!)

What would make possible the convergence of these two worldwide activities? A unified world—complete with other worldwide elements, such as all nations accessible for entrance and a universally understood language. It would also require a people with the conviction, courage and plan to take the gospel to the entire world. Do we not have these things presently in hand? Yes, or something very close to it. Are we living in the "last days" before the coming of Christ? Maybe. And maybe not. Only God knows for sure. But I pray that we are, for then our present mission will have placed us squarely in the midst of this prophecy!

Such a prospect may sound thrilling, and it is, but keep in mind the consequences of such an accomplishment. The price once paid for the carrying out of Christ's mission was enormous. We are being naive if we think the ultimate price in our day for the same mission will end up being substantially different. As our early brothers and sisters were unwilling to shrink back from the task in spite of the consequences, let us be willing to follow in the same path. We must all have the heart to shout, "Preach the Word, and bring it on! Amen!"

? Did you have any concept of the "thousand-year reign" prior to this study? If so, what was it? How have your views about the second coming of Christ and the end of the world been altered as a result of this study? Has this particular study appealed more to your intellect or more to your heart? Explain.

The Great White Throne of Judgment (20:11-15)

> *[11]Then I saw a great white throne and him who was seated on it. Earth and sky fled from his presence, and there was no place for them. [12]And I saw the dead, great and small, standing before the throne, and books were opened. Another book was opened, which is the book of life. The dead were judged according to what they had done as recorded in the books. [13]The sea gave up the dead that were in it, and death and Hades gave up the dead that were in them, and each person was judged according to what he had done. [14]Then death and Hades were thrown into the lake of fire. The lake of fire is the second death. [15]If anyone's name was not found written in the book of life, he was thrown into the lake of fire.*

Now, it would seem, comes the final Judgment Day. Heaven and earth fled away—the physical universe is gone (2 Peter 3:10-13, Hebrews 1:10-12, Revelation 21:1). The dead appear before the throne and books were opened, a reference to the deeds of each person. Those whose names are written in the book of life will enter heaven, and those whose names are omitted will be thrown into hell. The thought of such a day strikes terror into the hearts of almost anyone who will spend time contemplating it. Most people refuse even to think about it. But we cannot afford to be ignorant about our ultimate destiny. Therefore, let's take a few minutes to check out some pertinent verses on the subject.

There is a type of judgment which occurs at the point of physical death. Hebrews 9:27 speaks of it in these words: "...man is destined to die once, and after that to face judgment." On the other hand, Revelation 20 is one of several in-depth scriptures which describe the final Judgment Day. The other key passages are Acts 17 and Matthew 25. To provide a more complete picture of what to expect on that Great Day, both are included here. We need to read them carefully.

"*Therefore since we are God's offspring, we should not think that the divine being is like gold or silver or stone—an image made by man's design and skill. In the past God overlooked such ignorance, but now he commands all people everywhere to repent. For he has set a day when he will judge the world with justice by the man he has appointed. He has given proof of this to all men by raising him from the dead.*" (Acts 17:29-31)

"*When the Son of Man comes in his glory, and all the angels with him, he will sit on his throne in heavenly glory. All the nations will be gathered before him, and he will separate the people one from another as a shepherd separates the sheep from the goats. He will put the sheep on his right and the goats on his left.*

"*Then the King will say to those on his right, 'Come, you who are blessed by my Father; take your inheritance, the kingdom prepared for you since the creation of the world. For I was hungry and you gave me something to eat, I was thirsty and you gave me something to drink, I was a stranger and you invited me in, I needed clothes and you clothed me, I was sick and you looked after me, I was in prison and you came to visit me.'*

"*Then the righteous will answer him, 'Lord, when did we see you hungry and feed you, or thirsty and give you something to drink? When did we see you a stranger and invite you in, or needing clothes and clothe you? When did we see you sick or in prison and go to visit you?'*

"*The King will reply, 'I tell you the truth, whatever you did for one of the least of these brothers of mine, you did for me.'*

> *"Then he will say to those on his left, 'Depart from me, you who are cursed, into the eternal fire prepared for the devil and his angels. For I was hungry and you gave me nothing to eat, I was thirsty and you gave me nothing to drink, I was a stranger and you did not invite me in, I needed clothes and you did not clothe me, I was sick and in prison and you did not look after me.'*
>
> *"They also will answer, 'Lord, when did we see you hungry or thirsty or a stranger or needing clothes or sick or in prison, and did not help you?'*
>
> *"He will reply, 'I tell you the truth, whatever you did not do for one of the least of these, you did not do for me.'*
>
> *"Then they will go away to eternal punishment, but the righteous to eternal life." (Matthew 25:31-46)*

In Acts 17, several conclusions are clear. One, God commands repentance. Biblically, repentance is *not* sorrow, but the right kind of sorrow produces it (2 Corinthians 7:10). It is thus a change of mind which leads to a change in actions—a move away from sin and a move toward righteousness. Notice that *all* are to repent. In Jesus' ministry, some of the ones most needing repentance were the religious. The same is true in our day. Being religious does not make a person right with God. Doing the will of God as it is defined in the Bible is the only thing that will make us right (Matthew 7:21). Repentance must be a daily part of our life, for it is included in walking in the light and being continually cleansed by the blood of Christ (1 John 1:7-10).

Two, the certainty of Judgment is designed to motivate us to repent. The Holy Spirit came to convict the world of Judgment (John 16:7-8). Proverbs 1:7 says "The fear of the LORD is the beginning of knowledge." After we repent and get baptized (Acts 2:38), our motivation should be based more and more on the love of God, but we will never outgrow the need to be motivated by the reverent fear of God and the day he has appointed. The resurrection of Jesus is the guarantee given in this text that the Judgment Day will certainly come.

Three, the world will be judged in justice by Jesus Christ. For God to judge with justice means that he will judge *without* favoritism. Peter had this to say about this principle: "Since you call on a Father who judges each man's work impartially, live your lives as strangers here in reverent fear" (1 Peter 1:17).

For him to judge us by Jesus means that we will be held accountable for imitating his example (1 John 2:6). Many people have a quite distorted view of what "Christlikeness" actually is. It is not just being a nice, sweet person. He never was accused of such. He was an absolute radical about doing the will of God by living righteously and staying focused on his mission of seeking and saving the lost (Luke 19:10). We will be judged by his example and by his words—Christians and non-Christians alike (James 2:12 and John 12:48, respectively).

The emphasis in Matthew 25 is very convicting. Jesus does not deal with the matters we would naturally expect. He does not mention baptism, church attendance, financial contributions to the church, sharing our faith, studying with people and baptizing them, nor a host of other things that could have been mentioned. This is not to say that all of these things are unimportant or unessential. But since love for God and love for our fellow man are the supreme commands in the law (Matthew 22:36-40), our practice of them will be examined closely.

What lessons should we learn from this passage in Matthew 25? One, the things Jesus asks about are simple things, not requiring a high IQ or stellar talents. All that they require is heart. Simple enough. Feeding people, visiting those sick and in prison and clothing the needy are activities focused on loving the poor, those less fortunate than we are. How comfortable do you feel answering God about how much love you have had for these kinds of people?

Two, according to the wording of the passage, the righteousness of the sheep was an issue of character more than of actions. When Jesus commended them for their love, they did not remember doing their deeds. Their hearts were such that they had done these things naturally and not made a big issue of their service. It was what they *were*, not simply what they *did*. We must ask ourselves how natural it has become for us to serve the poor. Perhaps a more basic question is, are we doing it at all—even out of a sense of duty. Are you ready for a Matthew 25 Judgment Day?

Three, what we do for others is, in effect, done for Jesus. When Paul was persecuting Christians, he was persecuting Jesus (Acts 9:4). When we show love for the poor in the manner described in Matthew 25, we are showing love to Jesus, and when we are not serving in this manner, we are not serving Jesus. He takes how we treat others very personally. As John put it in 1 John 4:20:

> *If anyone says, "I love God," yet hates his brother, he is a*
> *liar. For anyone who does not love his brother, whom he has*
> *seen, cannot love God, whom he has not seen.*

Love for God is demonstrated in loving others, and love for others grows out of our love for God.

In our Revelation 20 Judgment scene, we see that the dead are judged according to their works. The issues surrounding the judgment of all men by their works are of paramount importance. For those outside of a saved relationship with Christ, every sin they commit will be recorded and brought up on the day of Judgment. They will be judged by the things done while in the body (2 Corinthians 5:10); by every idle word spoken (Matthew 12:36-37); and by their thoughts, motives and secrets (Romans 2:16, 1 Corinthians 4:5). Given the breadth of this examination, the thought of meeting God unforgiven is absolutely terrifying! Can you imagine all of your sins being broadcast on a giant screen in vivid detail for everyone who has ever lived to view? There is a way to avoid such an experience. Read on.

For the disciple, the thought of Judgment is sobering but should not be scary. In fact, John said in another of his writings, "There is no fear in love. But perfect love drives out fear, because fear has to do with punishment. The one who fears is not made perfect in love" (1 John 4:18). How can we avoid having the wrong kind of fear in facing God as our ultimate Judge? By living the totally committed life he calls for and by trusting his promises. Total commitment is not perfection, but rather faithfulness. It is the perfect commitment of an imperfect life. When we are walking in the light of his Word, we receive continual forgiveness (1 John 1:5-10), and none of our sins are held against us. Paul could not have said it more plainly than in Romans 4:8, which reads: "Blessed is the man whose sin the Lord will never count against him."

Then in what way will the Christian be judged by works? Again, John's writing can help us understand the issues. In John 6:28-29, he recorded the typical question of religious people (especially legalistic ones), and the response of Jesus.

> *Then they asked him, "What must we do to do the works*
> *God requires?"*
>   *Jesus answered, "The work of God is this: to believe in the*
> *one he has sent."*

In other words, the works by which we shall be judged are those associated with our faithful following of him as the Lord of our everyday lives. Such a follower has all of his sins wiped out (Acts 3:19), to be remembered by God no more (Hebrews 8:12). Now that is a message of grace, isn't it? We must just make sure grace is always our motivation for wholehearted service to God like it was for Paul (1 Corinthians 15:10) and that it is never an excuse for sinning (Romans 6:1-2). Remember that while God's grace is *freely* given, it has never been *cheaply* given. Let us love him, serve him, and face Judgment with confidence!

When the Judgment is complete, death and Hades will be cast into lake of fire (20:14-15). Did not Paul tell us that the last enemy to be destroyed is death? (1 Corinthians 15:26). Before that white throne, good and bad alike will find out the answers to all the spiritual questions about which they have wondered. Before that great throne, every knee will bow and every tongue will confess (Philippians 2:9-11). For those who are saved, the confession will be made with extreme joy and exhilaration. For those who are lost, it will be made with a bitter wail that mortals can now only imagine. The grand moment toward which the world has been speeding since its creation will finally arrive! We need to praise God and get ready!

? What about the relationship between grace and works causes you the most difficulty? Some people tend to be more "deceived" and others tend to be more "accused." What is the difference between the two types in how they view themselves and God? Which type are you? How does your tendency in this area affect your view of yourself? Other people? God?

15

▼

Home At Last!
REVELATION 21 AND 22

Finally—home at last! The beauties and joys of heaven are incomprehensible to the human mind at this time. The words of 1 Corinthians 2:9 in context are applied to the joys of receiving the gospel message, but how much more appropriate they are to describe the joys of being saved eternally by that message: "No eye has seen, no ear has heard, no mind has conceived what God has prepared for those who love him." Peter describes the blessings of heaven as an inheritance that "can never perish, spoil or fade—kept in heaven for you" (1 Peter 1:4). The level of joy experienced the first moment we see God will never diminish in the least. Nothing good will ever lessen and nothing bad will ever be present. It *sounds* far too good to be true, and it would *be* too good to be true, except for the God whose love exceeds any description which could be given by men or by angels. Because of who he is and whose we are, heaven exists and is now awaiting our arrival. Praise God! And now on to Revelation 21 and 22 which give us a window through which we can catch a glimpse of that new and amazing life.

At this point, we should note that the descriptions used are still symbolic, and therefore figurative, but the heart issues depicted are real. Some of the symbolism is borrowed from the latter part of Isaiah (Isaiah 65:17-19, 66:19-24) which describes the renewal of Israel after captivity. Because of this usage in Isaiah, some would apply the wording of Revelation 21 and 22 to the church on earth after it had been delivered from persecution. But keep in mind that borrowing wording from OT passages does not mean that the applications are identical. The overall context and flow would make an application to eternity much more reasonable in this last part of Revelation.

There is compelling evidence that this portion of Scripture is describing eternity and not simply a church delivered from Roman persecution. Several issues persuade me of this position. One is the sequence in Revelation thus far. After the destruction of Satan's allies was pictured, Satan himself was destroyed. If the book had skipped from chapter 19 to chapter 21, the delivered-church theory would make more sense. In other words, if the church was simply delivered from the persecutors (the three allies), and not Satan also, this view would seem more logical. But as it is, it does not. Revelation 20 goes too far in its description of the end of Satan and the Judgment Day for us to accept such a limited theory.

Two, the destruction of Satan, death and Hades, and the graphic portrayal of what appears to be a final Judgment in Revelation 20:10-15 seems *very* final. If God wanted to show us the end of time, he could not have found better words with which to do it. The wording of Revelation 21 seems not only to be graphic, but specific in describing life "on the other side."

Three, the fact that Revelation is God's last prophecy to man would seem to logically warrant a picture of the end of time, for in Genesis, we find Paradise lost, and in Revelation, we find Paradise restored. If the last part of Revelation were merely descriptive of a delivered church on earth, it seems that its length would constitute somewhat of an overkill. No other picture of deliverance in the book uses as much ink. On the other hand, if the final section is picturing eternity with God, it makes perfect sense.

In all fairness, we must note that Revelation 22:6-13 uses terminology clearly connected to the ending of persecution: 22:6 speaks of things that "must soon take place"; 22:10 tells us "the time is near"; and in 22:12 Jesus says, "I am coming soon" (in temporal judgment—1:7, 3:11). Obviously, these phrases must be applied to the events surrounding the Roman persecution. What about this issue? My thought is that since the book was, to a large extent, about the persecutors being defeated, John wanted to leave the readers focused on the realities about which the bulk of the book was written. That would be a natural thing to do. In this way, the book could conclude with the end of time, but also issue a final warning to stay focused on what had to be faced and overcome *in* time.

The Destiny of the Redeemed

Perfect Fellowship with God (21:1-8)

> *²¹:¹Then I saw a new heaven and a new earth, for the first heaven and the first earth had passed away, and there was no longer any sea. ²I saw the Holy City, the new Jerusalem, coming down out of heaven from God, prepared as a bride beautifully dressed for her husband. ³And I heard a loud voice from the throne saying, "Now the dwelling of God is with men, and he will live with them. They will be his people, and God himself will be with them and be their God. ⁴He will wipe every tear from their eyes. There will be no more death or mourning or crying or pain, for the old order of things has passed away."*
>
> *⁵He who was seated on the throne said, "I am making everything new!" Then he said, "Write this down, for these words are trustworthy and true."*
>
> *⁶He said to me: "It is done. I am the Alpha and the Omega, the Beginning and the End. To him who is thirsty I will give to drink without cost from the spring of the water of life. ⁷He who overcomes will inherit all this, and I will be his God and he will be my son. ⁸But the cowardly, the unbelieving, the vile, the murderers, the sexually immoral, those who practice magic arts, the idolaters and all liars—their place will be in the fiery lake of burning sulfur. This is the second death."*

The new heaven and new earth signify simply a new habitation. What it will really be like, we do not know. Certainly it will not be anything like the habitation in which we now live, for *we* will be so far different:

> *Dear friends, now we are children of God, and what we will be has not yet been made known. But we know that when he appears, we shall be like him, for we shall see him as he is (1 John 3:2).*

Peter wrote about our new environment in a similar way to Revelation 21:1:

> *But the day of the Lord will come like a thief. The heavens will disappear with a roar; the elements will be destroyed by fire, and the earth and everything in it will be laid bare.*
>
> *Since everything will be destroyed in this way, what kind of people ought you to be? You ought to live holy and godly*

lives as you look forward to the day of God and speed its coming. That day will bring about the destruction of the heavens by fire, and the elements will melt in the heat. But in keeping with his promise we are looking forward to a new heaven and a new earth, the home of righteousness. (2 Peter 3:10-13)

The end of the sea marks the end of man's separation from God, as also indicated in 4:6 and 15:2. God no longer lives in light unapproachable, for the redeemed have assumed their new bodies (whatever they may be like—2 Corinthians 5:1-4) and thus are equipped enjoy intimate fellowship with God. The new Jerusalem coming down out of heaven indicates the vision approaching John, not the church itself descending from heaven (as the rapturists might argue). The evil empire was described as a great city (Babylon) and now God's empire is described as the greatest city. The church also is pictured as a bride prepared to meet Jesus, demonstrating how effectively he was able to accomplish his goal "to present her to himself as a radiant church, without stain or wrinkle or any other blemish, but holy and blameless" (Ephesians 5:27).

The perfect state of heaven is described in 21:3-7. Perhaps the most comforting part of the passage is 21:4, which promises an end to emotional pain with its attendant mourning and tears. Life is punctuated with pain. The Psalmist captured that reality well with this description: "The length of our days is seventy years—or eighty, if we have the strength; yet their span is but trouble and sorrow, for they quickly pass, and we fly away" (Psalm 90:10).

For about a year, I walked and prayed in a cemetery very near where we lived at the time. It was a peaceful spot for undisturbed prayer sessions with God. Occasionally I read the epitaphs on the tombstones and found myself picturing the graveside services and the sorrows accompanying them. Once I had the thought of how much sorrow would have been felt had all of the burials taken place at the same time. Can you just imagine the combined pain which would have accompanied such a day? Now multiply that amount of pain by the thousands and thousands of burial places all over the world. The promise of no more emotional distress is wonderful beyond comprehension.

The roll call of hell is found in 21:8. Most of the sins on the list seem obvious enough to us, but the first one, cowardice may not be. We typically condone that character trait, viewing it as fairly normal and understandable. God, however, has another way of looking at it! All of us are fearful in certain circumstances, which is not sinful in itself, but giving into the fears *is* sin. Even Paul sometimes preached the Word "in weakness and fear, and with much trembling" (1 Corinthians 2:3). But God warned him not to let his fears deter him from his mission:

> *One night the Lord spoke to Paul in a vision: "Do not be afraid; keep on speaking, do not be silent. For I am with you, and no one is going to attack and harm you, because I have many people in this city." So Paul stayed for a year and a half, teaching them the word of God. (Acts 18:9-11)*

Paul experienced *serious* persecution sharing the message of Christ. Read 2 Corinthians 11:23-29 to see the extent of it. However, even when preaching carried such inherent dangers, he was not thereby excused from proclaming it. When Jesus spoke of the responsibility of every disciple to proclaim the good news, he gave some sobering warnings:

> *"So do not be afraid of them. There is nothing concealed that will not be disclosed, or hidden that will not be made known. What I tell you in the dark, speak in the daylight; what is whispered in your ear, proclaim from the roofs. Do not be afraid of those who kill the body but cannot kill the soul. Rather, be afraid of the One who can destroy both soul and body in hell. Are not two sparrows sold for a penny? Yet not one of them will fall to the ground apart from the will of your Father. And even the very hairs of your head are all numbered. So don't be afraid; you are worth more than many sparrows.*
>
> *"Whoever acknowledges me before men, I will also acknowledge him before my Father in heaven. But whoever disowns me before men, I will disown him before my Father in heaven." (Matthew 10:26-33)*

Paul was threatened with emotional and physical persecution, while we typically face only the emotional. Frequently we are most frightened by the thought that we will be considered *weird* by those with whom we share. Our people-pleasing, conflict-avoiding natures cause us to want to "fit in" or "blend in" with those around us. Perish the thought that we would stand out! But the very definition of a disciple demands that we stand out from the crowd. God's people have always been, and will always be, the small minority. Therefore, we will always be different from those around us.

Think back through your life and remember the people who most influenced you or who were most admired by you. Were they the "blend in" type or the "stand out" type? The answer is obvious, isn't it? We had all better quit worrying about what men think about us and concentrate on what God thinks! And we had better wonder what men will think of us on the Day of Judgment rather than what they may think in this life!

"The second death," mentioned in 21:8, is equated with being cast into hell. The basic meaning of death is separation. James 2:26 mentions that the body without the spirit is dead. Thus, physical death occurs when the spirit is separated from the body in which it resides. The second death is man's separation from his Maker. 2 Thessalonians 1:9 describes this spiritual separation in these words: "They will be punished with everlasting destruction and shut out from the presence of the Lord and from the majesty of his power." In this life, no person has any idea of what being separated totally from God will be like. Of course, there is a type of spiritual separation due to sin (Isaiah 59:1-2), but even in this situation, God still "causes his sun to rise on the evil and the good, and sends rain on the righteous and the unrighteous" (Matthew 5:45). The final and irreversible chasm between God and man will be horrible beyond description, the "blackest darkness" (2 Peter 2:17).

Perfect Protection by God (21:9-27)

> ⁹One of the seven angels who had the seven bowls full of the seven last plagues came and said to me, "Come, I will show you the bride, the wife of the Lamb." ¹⁰And he carried me away in the Spirit to a mountain great and high, and showed me the Holy City, Jerusalem, coming down out of heaven from God. ¹¹It shone with the glory of God, and its brilliance was like that of a very precious jewel, like a jasper, clear as crystal. ¹²It had a great, high wall with twelve gates, and with twelve angels at the gates. On the gates were written the names of the

twelve tribes of Israel. ¹³There were three gates on the east, three on the north, three on the south and three on the west. ¹⁴The wall of the city had twelve foundations, and on them were the names of the twelve apostles of the Lamb.

¹⁵The angel who talked with me had a measuring rod of gold to measure the city, its gates and its walls. ¹⁶The city was laid out like a square, as long as it was wide. He measured the city with the rod and found it to be 12,000 stadia in length, and as wide and high as it is long. ¹⁷He measured its wall and it was 144 cubits thick, by man's measurement, which the angel was using. ¹⁸The wall was made of jasper, and the city of pure gold, as pure as glass. ¹⁹The foundations of the city walls were decorated with every kind of precious stone. The first foundation was jasper, the second sapphire, the third chalcedony, the fourth emerald, ²⁰the fifth sardonyx, the sixth carnelian, the seventh chrysolite, the eighth beryl, the ninth topaz, the tenth chrysoprase, the eleventh jacinth, and the twelfth amethyst. ²¹The twelve gates were twelve pearls, each gate made of a single pearl. The great street of the city was of pure gold, like transparent glass.

²²I did not see a temple in the city, because the Lord God Almighty and the Lamb are its temple. ²³The city does not need the sun or the moon to shine on it, for the glory of God gives it light, and the Lamb is its lamp. ²⁴The nations will walk by its light, and the kings of the earth will bring their splendor into it. ²⁵On no day will its gates ever be shut, for there will be no night there. ²⁶The glory and honor of the nations will be brought into it. ²⁷Nothing impure will ever enter it, nor will anyone who does what is shameful or deceitful, but only those whose names are written in the Lamb's book of life.

The picture now goes back to the idea introduced in the first two verses of chapter 21. John continues his description of the vision of heaven which he was seeing. For God to describe heaven to us, he had to use figures which suggested great value to man, such as costly stones, gold and other beautiful objects. Surely these things are not literal, but are used to convey the idea that heaven will be amazingly magnificent. Describing heaven to humans is much more difficult than trying to describe Paris to an infant. There simply are few points of reference. One thing is sure, given the activity and creativity of God, we can be sure we will not be sitting on the clouds strumming harps for eternity! No one will describe heaven as boring. Our lives in eternity will be unimaginably wonderful, with every moment filled with the exhilaration of a joy that never fades (1 Peter 1:4). Once Paul got a glimpse of it (2 Corinthians 12:2-4), he knew death was "better by far" than continuing to live on this earth with its limitations (Philippians 1:23).

A number of spiritual lessons can be gleaned from this highly figurative passage. The new Jerusalem (21:10) will be lit with the brilliance of the presence of God and his Lamb (21:23). God dwelling in us as saved humans lights up our lives in innumerable ways, but we will then *dwell* in the very presence of God.

The mention of the nations in 21:24, 26 conveys the amazing thought that the relatively small band of persecuted disciples made their mark on the whole world. The small and the great from every tribe, people, language and nation are able to enter the eternal kingdom because of the faithful fulfillment of the Great Commission.

The twelve gates (21:12) suggest that the redeemed "will receive a rich welcome into the eternal kingdom of our Lord and Savior Jesus Christ" (2 Peter 1:11). The angels at the gates provide a contrast to Genesis 3:23-24, where an angel kept man from entering the Garden of Eden after he had sinned. The twelve gates of pearl may be intended to suggest the extreme value of having suffered and overcome, for pearls are the one type of precious stone formed by pain and suffering. The entire vision suggests great peace and joy to the delivered soul, which in victory must cry "I made it—praise God!"

Perfect Provisions from God (22:1-5)

> [22:1]*Then the angel showed me the river of the water of life, as clear as crystal, flowing from the throne of God and of the Lamb* [2]*down the middle of the great street of the city. On each side of the river stood the tree of life, bearing twelve crops of fruit, yielding its fruit every month. And the leaves of the tree are for the healing of the nations.* [3]*No longer will there be any curse. The throne of God and of the Lamb will be in the city, and his servants will serve him.* [4]*They will see his face, and his name will be on their foreheads.* [5]*There will be no more night. They will not need the light of a lamp or the light of the sun, for the Lord God will give them light. And they will reign for ever and ever.*

Revelation 22 begins with a picture of the tree of life lost in the paradise of Eden by the sin of Adam and Eve, it is found in the paradise of God by the grace of Jesus Christ. The cursed earth, full of thorns and thistles (Genesis 3:17-19), gives way to heaven, where the trees always bloom in the city of God. In this life, we reign gratefully in the presence of struggles, but there we reign gleefully in the absence of struggles. And most importantly, we will see him face to face. When Moses wanted to see God, he was told "you cannot see my face, for no one may see me and live" (Exodus 33:20). We will finally have the inexpressible joy of seeing the One who shed his blood that we might ultimately enjoy sweet fellowship with him while the ages roll on, world without end!

? How would you have described heaven in the past? How would you describe it now? What about the description in Revelation 21 helps you the most? In what ways will a great desire to go to heaven influence your life on earth? How can you enhance your desire to go to heaven?

The Concluding Warnings (22:6-21)

⁶The angel said to me, "These words are trustworthy and true. The Lord, the God of the spirits of the prophets, sent his angel to show his servants the things that must soon take place."

⁷"Behold, I am coming soon! Blessed is he who keeps the words of the prophecy in this book."

⁸I, John, am the one who heard and saw these things. And when I had heard and seen them, I fell down to worship at the feet of the angel who had been showing them to me. ⁹But he said to me, "Do not do it! I am a fellow servant with you and with your brothers the prophets and of all who keep the words of this book. Worship God!"
¹⁰Then he told me, "Do not seal up the words of the prophecy of this book, because the time is near. ¹¹Let him who does wrong continue to do wrong; let him who is vile continue to be vile; let him who does right continue to do right; and let him who is holy continue to be holy."

¹²"Behold, I am coming soon! My reward is with me, and I will give to everyone according to what he has done. ¹³I am the Alpha and the Omega, the First and the Last, the Beginning and the End.

[14]"Blessed are those who wash their robes, that they may have the right to the tree of life and may go through the gates into the city. [15]Outside are the dogs, those who practice magic arts, the sexually immoral, the murderers, the idolaters and everyone who loves and practices falsehood.

[16]"I, Jesus, have sent my angel to give you this testimony for the churches. I am the Root and the Offspring of David, and the bright Morning Star."

[17]The Spirit and the bride say, "Come!" And let him who hears say, "Come!" Whoever is thirsty, let him come; and whoever wishes, let him take the free gift of the water of life.

[18]I warn everyone who hears the words of the prophecy of this book: If anyone adds anything to them, God will add to him the plagues described in this book. [19]And if anyone takes words away from this book of prophecy, God will take away from him his share in the tree of life and in the holy city, which are described in this book.

[20]He who testifies to these things says, "Yes, I am coming soon."

Amen. Come, Lord Jesus.

[21]The grace of the Lord Jesus be with God's people. Amen.

In this concluding section, John addresses the pressing issues facing the disciples of his time. It was a very serious situation they were in, making essential the final warnings contained in the passage. Several "last things" in Revelation are found in this final section of the Bible. In 22:14, we find the last blessing and last beatitude; in 22:17, the last invitation; in 22:18-19, the last warning; and in 22:20, the last promise and the last prayer.

The last invitation (22:17) is brief but powerful. The Holy Spirit, who inspired the word of God, offers the invitation to the world. The bride of Christ, the church, adds in its voice as it takes the Great Commission to every nation. Individual disciples, as they hear and respond, now add their offer of the good news to others. Anyone who has a hunger and thirst for righteousness, or who is willing to develop that spiritual appetite, may come. Everyone who wishes can come to God through the sacrifice of Christ, and receive his free gift of life.

Evangelism is the heart of God, Christ and the Holy Spirit. In ever-increasing ways, it must be the heart of every disciple. Our world is sin-sick and under condemnation. We must be as urgent to spread the gospel as Jesus is. Time is short. We can't waste it. We must make every day count and seize every opportunity.

The last warning is reminiscent of similar warnings near the beginning of the Bible (Deuteronomy 4:2) and near the middle (Proverbs 30:5-6). The message in these three passages is that man does not sit in judgment of the Word to determine its validity; the Word sits in judgment of man to determine his destiny!

The last prayer (22:20) is very simple: "Come, Lord Jesus!" It is the prayer of a man deeply in love with his Lord and anxious to see him and be with him. (See 1 Corinthians 16:22.) Is that your prayer? Are you ready to live the life of a disciple every day; to share the message disciples share, every day; to face the rejection and persecution of those who do not understand nor appreciate that message; and to pay the ultimate price of your own blood if need be in order to make Jesus truly the Lord of your life? The price of discipleship is everything we have and are, and everything we ever hope to have and be. Walking the path Jesus did was not easy for him. It was not easy for the first century church. It is not easy in our day. It will *never* be easy! But it will be abundantly worth it! And *that* is the message of Revelation. We must accept it and let it change our lives, to the glory of Almighty God!

The book of Revelation reveals Jesus Christ in all his power and might. In this work the cosmic curtain is pulled back, and we clearly see him who is the Alpha and the Omega. We see his enemies, and we see his superiority to them *all*. Once we are in his presence, we will fall down like the multitudes pictured in this book, and we will cry out with a passion we did not know we had, "Mine eyes have seen the glory!"

? Would you like to make sure you have gained everything from this study of Revelation that God intended? Then spend an extended period of uninterrupted time and write out your answers to the following questions: What *facts* have you learned from the study? What spiritual *lessons* have you learned? What did you learn about your own heart? What did you learn about God? What did you learn about Satan? What did you learn about the mission of God's kingdom?

Epilogue

▼

After reading books of this nature, I sometimes wonder how the material discussed affected the author who spent a good deal of time pulling it all together. Was this just an interesting academic exercise for him, or was his own life changed in some way by what he studied? In case you are wondering these things about your present author, I would like to offer a few final thoughts.

For one thing, I can say that I have come away from my study of Revelation completely impressed with God. He is absolute love, willing to pay any price for the redemption of his creatures. God is also absolute justice, and a study of Revelation demonstrates this attribute like no other portion of Scripture. He abhors sin in any form and in any person. He withholds nothing in his pursuit of the souls of men, but neither does he withhold anything in the punishment of those who resist his overtures of love. His love and justice meet at the cross, we often say, but they are not as easy to reconcile in other settings. By faith we accept all that we understand about his love and justice while we plead for more understanding. As we plead, we must continue to study, for it is in Scripture that he is most fully revealed.

In one sense, the more we learn about God, the less we may feel we know about him. When we stand a distance from a window, we may not see a very large part of what lies on the other side of it. However, the closer we get to it, the bigger the view becomes. Similarly, the more we see of God, the more we realize how much we do not yet see! And we are left with the realization that seeking an understanding of him is a lifetime proposition.

In spite of gaining many answers about God and his plan from my study, I am left with a few soul-searching questions. They are mainly questions of application. What will we do in our pampered generation if persecution takes on physical implications? What will *I* do? The book of Revelation is not a fairy tale about "Never-Never Land." It is a book about reality—the reality of life and death, sin and judgment, heaven and hell. As we observe remarkable progress in the spread of the gospel throughout the world, we must be aware of the price tag for such an accomplishment.

Our age is an exceedingly wicked one. The same sins have always been practiced, true enough, but now they are blatantly practiced. Sins such as homosexuality and abortion are being increasingly accepted in society. In America, we are fast approaching the point where a majority views these actions as morally acceptable. When the darkness becomes more and more pervasive, the light shines brightest. But the light also becomes a clearer target to those who hate it. And "hate" is the correct word to use. "Blessed are you when men hate you, when they exclude you and insult you and reject your name as evil, because of the Son of Man" (Luke 6:22). "But I tell you who hear me: Love your enemies, do good to those who hate you" (Luke 6:27). "All men will hate you because of me" (Luke 21:17).

As I conclude this exposition, I am left to marvel at God, his plan for the universe, the magnitude of the spiritual battle, its certain conclusion, and the eternal home prepared by Jesus for his people. He is truly the Lord of lords and the King of kings. With him reigning on the throne of the universe, his loyal followers have nothing to fear. Whatever man may do to us, he cannot kill our souls. Only God can cast both body and soul into hell (Matthew 10:28) and if we are disciples, God is for us not against us (see Romans 8:31-39). Therefore, we can relax and enjoy our relationship with him, knowing that even intense persecution cannot do us ultimate harm.

John repeatedly was filled with overwhelming amazement when he received and wrote the visions given to him. May we remain amazed as we lift up our eyes to catch a glimpse of our Lord's majesty, seated on his eternal throne "far above all rule and authority, power and dominion, and every title that can be given, not only in the present age but also in the one to come" (Ephesians 1:21). From this day forward, let us determine to live every day with the deepest of convictions that "Mine eyes have seen his glory!" With that vision let us live, and with that vision let us die.

Appendix 1

▼

The Premillennial Doctrine

I was exposed to the basic futurist teaching as a young person and accepted it as being true for many years. I did not know an alternative was available, and being Biblically ignorant, saw no reason to question what I was taught. However, I did not like the impact it had on the leaders who taught it. They often seemed to be *caught up* in it to the point that they lost perspective of the average person's needs for practical help in trying to live a spiritual life in a pagan society. They were more intrigued by trying to figure out dates and events of the "end times" than about how the world could be evangelized for Christ. My present opinion is that people have become materialistic to the point that they cannot envision anything good apart from this earth, including heaven! Also, the futurist teaching appeals to the emotions because of its "mysterious" elements, and many people are looking for mystical fancy rather than Biblical fact.

When I began to study the Bible in depth on the topic of premillennialism, I soon saw the vast inconsistencies in the teaching. I have read many writings on all sides of the issue, and have no doubt that my earlier indoctrination in premillennialism was not correct. Exciting it was, but accurate it was not! This view removes the book from its original setting of Christians being persecuted and killed in the early centuries of the church. What comfort would a "twentieth-century newspaper" type of prophecy bring to people being killed for their faith? Such an approach is filled with distortions of Scripture, and fanciful interpretations cooked with a "dash" of Ezekiel, a "shake" of Daniel, "scoops" of Revelation and "pinches" from other NT books. In spite of its popularity, the view has little to commend it from a Biblical perspective and many reasons to reject it.

The Reign of Christ

The premillennialists claim that Jesus will not begin his reign until the time of his return (second coming). He will then reign on a literal throne in a literal Jerusalem for a literal one thousand years. When this concept is examined in light of OT prophecy about the Messiah and in his NT fulfillment, the idea is shown to be false.

Zechariah 6:12-13 is one of the key passages disproving the validity of premillenialism. For clarity, we will quote from the more literal New American Standard Version (NASV):

> *"Then say to him, 'Thus says the LORD of hosts, "Behold, a man whose name is Branch, for He will branch out from where He is; and He will build the temple of the LORD. Yes, it is He who will build the temple of the LORD, and He who will bear the honor and sit and rule on His throne. Thus, He will be a priest on His throne, and the counsel of peace will be between the two offices."'"*

The New Testament makes it clear that Jesus built his church, and that his church is God's temple (Matthew 16:18; 1 Corinthians 3:11, 16; 2 Corinthians 6:16; Ephesians 2:19-22). Now look back at the Zechariah passage in light of the church being the temple of God.

Christ would sit on his throne (Zechariah 6:13), and Acts 2:1, 32-35 says that he began occupying that throne on the Day of Pentecost when the church was established. He was to be a priest on his throne (Zechariah 6:13), and he is a priest now (Hebrews 4:14). This Branch was to rule on his throne while sitting (Zechariah 6:13), and he began sitting on this throne nearly two thousand years ago (Acts 2:32-35). Therefore, he is *ruling* on his throne now. Since he was said to be a priest on his throne, and he is a priest in heaven (Hebrews 4:14), his throne must be in heaven. In fact, he *cannot* be priest on earth, for Hebrews 8:4 says: "If he were on earth, he would not be a priest...." Therefore, his throne *cannot* be on earth.

Psalm 110:1, 4 also speaks of Christ ruling as a priest. In this case, his rule will last until his enemies are conquered. In 1 Corinthians 15:25-26 the Bible says, "For he must reign until he has put all his enemies under his feet. The last enemy to be destroyed is death." Therefore, Jesus is reigning now and will continue to do so until the resurrection of the dead, at which point he will *cease* to reign over the Messianic kingdom as heaven begins. This truth is exactly opposite to what the premillennial doctrine teaches. They say he will *begin* reigning at his return, and Paul says he will *cease*! It should be mentioned that as a part of Deity, he reigns over heaven and all of its subjects, which includes all of the redeemed from all ages.

It should be obvious that Jesus is reigning in his spiritual kingdom now. In his earthly ministry he claimed that the kingdom was *near* in fulfillment of prophecy (Daniel 2:44, Mark 1:15, Hebrews 12:28). This kingdom would come in the lifetime of some of the apostles and it would come with power (Mark 9:1). Power came when the Spirit came at Pentecost (Acts 1:8, 2:1-4). Therefore, the kingdom was established on the day of Pentecost. After this time, the kingdom is spoken of as a present reality (Colossians 1:13, 4:11, Revelation 1:6). Furthermore, the kingdom is equated with the church in Matthew 16:18-19. Any future view of the kingdom is of necessity referring to the heavenly state after it has been delivered up to the Father by Christ (1 Corinthians 15:24).

The Place of the Nation of Israel

Premillennialists typically place a good deal of emphasis on the role of Israel in "end time" prophesies. However, such an emphasis can easily be shown to be mistaken. One of the first questions needing an answer is this: Will there be a restoration of Israel in fulfillment of Biblical prophecy? The answer is *negative*, for several reasons.

- Christ is *already* on David's throne (Acts 2:30-33).
- The tent of David has been rebuilt (Acts 15:14-17). The saving of the Gentiles is in fulfillment of Amos 9:11-12, according to James, the Lord's brother. The argument in Acts 15 is clearly that the tent was to be rebuilt before the Gentiles were to "seek the Lord." Therefore, either the tent here is *spiritual* in nature, meaning the church, or Gentiles are yet in their sins and the Great Commission is nullified!
- God's promises to Israel concerning the land inheritance have all been fulfilled (Joshua 23:14). Notice that the

boundaries God specified to Abraham in Genesis 15:18 were reached by the time 1 Kings 4:21 and 2 Chronicles 9:26 were written.
- God said through Jeremiah that Israel could not be made whole again (Jeremiah 19:11).
- Jesus promised that the kingdom would be taken away from the Jews (Matthew 21:33-43).
- The last state of the Jews would be worse than the first (Matthew 12:43-45).
- God's special people are *spiritual* Jews (Christians) and not *physical* ones (Romans 2:28-29, 9:6; Galatians 3:26-29).

But what about Romans 11:25-26? Does it not clearly state "and so all Israel will be saved?" The larger context of the passage begins back in Romans 11:11. After establishing the fact that most physical Jews had always rejected God, Paul moves on to show how God intended to use even their *wrong* choices for good (Romans 11:11-24). Israel's wrong choices and subsequent rejection have ended up being a blessing to the Gentiles. They had Jesus crucified, making salvation available. They drove Christians out of Jerusalem, which resulted in the Gentiles being able to hear the gospel. They rejected the message in each city to which the early missionaries preached, after which they preached to the Gentiles (Acts 13:46). However, if the Jews' rejection of the gospel ended up blessing the world, then how much more their acceptance would do for the world! (Romans 11:15).

Next Paul expresses hope that the Gentiles' inclusion in God's kingdom will provoke the Jews to envy, causing them to reconsider the message of Christ (Romans 11:13-14). This section concludes with a warning to the Gentiles not to be prideful and self-righteous. They had not been a part of the olive root (Judaism) in the first place; they had been merely grafted in by the grace of God. The Jews had been cut off because of their faithless rejection of Christ, but they can be grafted back in again if they turn to Jesus in faith. How they might be motivated to respond in this way is discussed in the remainder of the chapter (Romans 11:25-36).

Israel's hardening is stated to be only "in part" until the "full number" of Gentiles has come in (Romans 11:25). Since it is *partial*, it has the possibility of being reversed. The key to a reversal is the coming in of the "full number of Gentiles." Paul likely was referring to the completion of his own ministry as the apostle to the Gentiles (Galatians 2:7), resulting in more and more Gentiles in the church all over the world. In Romans 15:24, we find that his missionary plans were far from completion, for he planned to go all the way to Spain. Once this larger Gentile inclusion had occurred, all Israel could be saved in the sense being discussed in this context.

The word "so" in Romans 11:26 is from the Greek *houtos*, an adverb of manner, meaning "in this way." "In this way" refers back to the *envy-provoking* process mentioned in Romans 11:13-14. (Paul refers to the same idea again in Romans 11:31). Therefore, when the Jews saw the growing number of Gentiles in the church of Jesus Christ, and the blessings from God that they were enjoying, those with good hearts would be envious enough to humble out and reconsider. In this way, they would be saved. The "all Israel" refers to those whose hearts would allow them to become humble and reconsider. It *could not* refer to every last Israelite coming to Christ at some future point—for a number of reasons.

For one thing, the "narrow road" will never be chosen by a majority from any nation, race, or population group (Matthew 7:13-14). This was true of the Jews even during their heyday, as the early part of Romans 11 establishes forcefully. Two, Paul had already expressed his hope that *some* would turn to Christ by being provoked to envy (Romans 11:14). Three, even if some future generation of Jews in the majority were to accept Christ, what comfort would that be to the scores of generations that had already died lost? Centuries have passed in which millions of Jews have rejected Christ and been lost as a result.

The key idea of "all Israel" being saved is that of hopeful *potential*, much like Jesus expressed in John 12:32 ("I...will draw *all men* to myself," emphasis added) and in John 13:35 ("By this *all men* will know that you are my disciples," emphasis added). Note that the quote in Romans 11:26-27 refers to salvation in Christ which became available at the cross and will continue to be available to anyone who will accept the gospel in faith. The only plan of salvation that God has and will have to the end of time is this plan, which must be accepted individually! (See Acts 4:8-12.) He still loves the rejecting Jews and desires to save them, for his promises made to the patriarchs still stand. But his salvation can be based on nothing less than the blood of Christ accepted by bowing our hearts and knees to his lordship.

The Second Coming of Christ

Our next consideration involves the second coming of Christ. When he comes, there will be only one bodily resurrection of the dead, as good and bad are raised simultaneously to be judged (John 5:28-29). All nations will be gathered for this great day (Matthew 25:31-34). Note that this is a judgment of every person within all nations, not a judgment of entire nations *as* nations, as some premillennialists claim. (Compare the wording of Matthew 25:32 with Matthew 28:19 in this regard.)

As stated in the first chapter of this book, there simply cannot be two separate bodily resurrections. If the righteous are raised on the "last day" (John 6:40), and the unrighteous are judged on the "last day" (John 12:48), both must occur at that time. We must allow the last day to really be *the last day*! When the last trumpet sounds, the dead are raised and the living are changed—in the twinkling of an eye, no less (1 Corinthians 15:51-52). If the wicked are raised a thousand years later, they will not be awakened by the last trumpet, for it will have already sounded! When it does sound, the physical universe will be destroyed (2 Peter 3:10-12, Revelation 21:1). Note that the OT passages which speak of the earth remaining "forever" mean only that it is "age-lasting." Ordinances such as circumcision and the Levitical priesthood with its sacrifices are also called "everlasting," but they are simply age-lasting (which in that case was the Mosaic Age).[1]

Even the "proof-text" for the premillennialist view of the rapture falls far short of actually teaching it:

> *For the Lord himself will come down from heaven, with a loud command, with the voice of the archangel and with the trumpet call of God, and the dead in Christ will rise first. After that, we who are still alive and are left will be* caught up *together with them in the clouds to meet the Lord in the air. And so we will be with the Lord forever. (1 Thessalonians 4:16-17, emphasis added)*

What about the passage would make anyone look for a rapture of the righteous to heaven for seven years, followed by a return to earth for a thousand years? The explanation seems simple enough—we will go to be with the Lord forever, rather than him coming to be with us on the earth. The futurists want him to come and be with them on our little planet, but Jesus wants his children to be with him in his amazing heaven.

Does It Really Matter?

A final consideration might be a look at the real dangers of the premillennial view. Surely no one would argue that salvation is based on a perfect understanding of Biblical prophecy! However, accepting the premillennial theories has some serious implications.

- Premillenial theory denies that Christ is reigning now, and therefore denies God's eternal purpose in Christ (Ephesians 3:10-11).
- It contradicts every passage which speaks of this present period as "the last days" (Acts 2:15-17, 1 Corinthians 10:11, Hebrews 1:1-2, 1 Peter 1:20).
- It makes Jesus false to his promises when he said that the kingdom was near (Mark 1:15).
- It alternates between Judaism and Christianity, by reviving the OT sacrificial system during the thousand year reign. However, that old covenant Jesus nailed to the cross (Colossians 2:14, Ephesians 2:15).
- It demotes Christ from the throne of his majesty to the earth, his footstool (Psalm 110:1).
- It denies that Amos 9:11-12 is fulfilled and thus, denies salvation to the Gentiles (Acts 15:14-17).
- It is the same mistake that the first century Jews made by expecting an earthly kingdom which was political in nature.

Paul said in Philippians 1:23 that he wanted to *go* be with the Lord, but the premillenialists in essence say, "Lord, you come be with us; we like it here." Jesus makes it plain in John 14:1-3 that eternal rewards have absolutely nothing to do with this earth:

"Do not let your hearts be troubled. Trust in God; trust also in me. In my Father's house are many rooms; if it were not so, I would have told you. I am going there to prepare a place for you. And if I go and prepare a place for you, I will come back and take you to be with me that you also may be where I am."

Appendix 2

▼

Matthew 24:
An End or *The* End?

Matthew 24 contains a significant amount of apocalyptic language and is written in such a manner that most who read it immediately assume that it is describing the second coming of Christ and the end of the world. Based on this assumption, certain phrases in this passage are widely considered to be synonymous with the second coming of Christ. For example, consider these verses:

> *"You will hear of wars and rumors of wars....Nation will rise against nation, and kingdom against kingdom. There will be famines and earthquakes in various places." (Matthew 24:6-7)*

> *"And this gospel of the kingdom will be preached in the whole world as a testimony to all nations, and then the end will come." (Matthew 24:14)*

To anyone who has heard much teaching on the subject of prophecy, this terminology has become familiar when speaking about the "end times."

However, a closer examination of Matthew 24 in context, along with the parallels in other accounts, reveals something quite different. An examination of these scriptures will convince the open-minded person that Jesus' words describe the destruction of Jerusalem in 70 AD rather than the end of the world. Since this passage is often misinterpreted and used in erroneous systems of doctrine, this appendix will provide an examination of it for those who want to dig deeper into prophetic studies regarding the second coming of Christ and the end of the world. The topic is, of necessity, one which demands deliberate, careful study. You will probably not read what is said here and immediately grasp the issues involved. The subject is too complex for that approach. You will have to study with an open Bible, open notebook and open mind. If you study this subject in this manner, you will be stimulated intellectually and rewarded with a much deeper understanding of Biblical prophecy.

Luke 21

Matthew's gospel was written with a Jewish audience in mind. Parts of it, including Matthew 24, present difficulties for those with a non-Jewish background. For this reason, it is better for us to begin with parallel passages in other gospels. Both Luke and Mark were likely written primarily with Gentile audiences in mind. (Note: Some of the details which occur in all three accounts will not be discussed fully until we come to the explanation of Matthew 24. Patience will be required.) Luke 21 gives us the fullest context out of which the apostles asked their key questions. Read this account carefully.

> *As he looked up, Jesus saw the rich putting their gifts into the temple treasury. He also saw a poor widow put in two very small copper coins. "I tell you the truth," he said, "this poor widow has put in more than all the others. All these people gave their gifts out of their wealth; but she out of her poverty put in all she had to live on."*
>
> *Some of his disciples were remarking about how the temple was adorned with beautiful stones and with gifts dedicated to God. But Jesus said, "As for what you see here, the time will come when not one stone will be left on another; every one of them will be thrown down."*
>
> *"Teacher," they asked, "when will these things happen? And what will be the sign that they are about to take place?"* (Luke 21:1-7)

The apostles were amazed and somewhat rebuffed by Jesus' comparison of the widow's giving to the giving of the rich. By contrast, the rich gave much larger amounts, but Jesus was much more impressed by her sacrifice. The apostles were quick to try to help Jesus get the bigger picture! After all, they explained, the temple with its beautiful stones was built with the gifts of the rich. They evidently thought that Jesus should have been more appreciative of the giving of the richer people. He replied that the temple was going to be totally destroyed.

That comment was *shocking* to them, which led to their two questions. They asked a "time" question (*when* would "these things" happen) and a "sign" question (what will be the *sign* that "they" [these things] are about to take place). In context, "these things" can be none other than the destruction of the temple. Both questions concern "these things" and not two separate events. If the second coming were the subject of Jesus' answers, he answered questions they did not ask, and Theophilus, to whom the book of Luke was addressed (1:3), would have been misled.

Now with Bible in hand, let's notice Jesus' answers to the apostles' two questions:

A. What the sign is *not* (Luke 21:8-19)
  1. False christs (21:8).
     Wars and revolutions (21:9). The "end" mentioned here is the end of Judaism marked by the destruction of the temple rather than the end of the world. (More on this point later.)
  2. Calamities of various types (21:10-11).
     Persecution (21:12-19). Can anyone doubt that these verses were fulfilled in the lives of the apostles?
B. What the sign *is* (21:20-24)
  1. The "abomination that causes desolation" found in Matthew 24:15 and Mark 13:14 is simplified in Luke 21:20. That is why we are studying Luke's account first—he keeps it simple for us Gentiles! When the Roman armies under Titus surrounded Jerusalem in 70 AD, the end of the city, the temple and Judaism was near, ensuring the actual desecration of the temple by Gentiles. (See Daniel 8:13, 9:27, 11:31, 12:11 for the original prophecy.)
  2. The wording of Luke 21:21-24 cannot possibly be applied to the second coming of Christ. Read these verses carefully and notice that they fit the destruction of the city perfectly.
  3. Note that the "time of punishment" in 21:22 is a *fulfillment* (see Daniel 9:24-27). Many passages in the Old Testament and New Testament prophecy

the destruction of Jerusalem, because by it Judaism was effectively terminated! Although Jewish practices continued in some form, the real heart of Judaism was based on the sacrificial system which ended and has never been revived.

C. The *time* question (21:25-33)

1. Apocalyptic language is used to show the judgment of God against a nation. (See Isaiah 13:6-13, 19:1, 34:2-8; Ezekiel 32:1-10; Joel 2:1-11, 28-32; Amos 8:9; Zephaniah 1:14-2:3.) The coming of the Son of Man does not have to be the second coming, but rather a coming in judgment. Just to make this point clear, look at Matthew 16:28 (the parallel to Mark 9:1, with which we are much more familiar): "I tell you the truth, some who are standing here will not taste death before they see the Son of Man coming in his kingdom." Whether the *coming* here is simply referring to the establishment of the church on the Day of Pentecost (Acts 2) or the coming in judgment against Jerusalem in 70 AD, it *cannot* be the second coming. God's coming in the entire Bible is more often a coming in judgment than any other type of "coming."

2. Fig-tree parable (21:29-31). Just as the presence of new leaves foretold the arrival of summer, the signs of which Jesus spoke announced his coming in judgment.

3. No specific time given, but the general time is within *one generation* of approximately 40 years (21:32). The wording clearly is applied to *all* "these things."

4. Therefore, they needed to *watch* for the sign (21:34-36).

Mark 13

Mark's account is quite similar, showing the same context of the widow's gift. Read Mark 12:41-44 to see the similarity. Then notice the comments and questions of the apostles in Mark 13:1-4:

> *As he was leaving the temple, one of his disciples said to him, "Look, Teacher! What massive stones! What magnificent buildings!"*
>
> *"Do you see all these great buildings?" replied Jesus. "Not one stone here will be left on another; every one will be thrown down."*
>
> *As Jesus was sitting on the Mount of Olives opposite the temple, Peter, James, John and Andrew asked him privately, "Tell us, when will these things happen? And what will be the sign that they are all about to be fulfilled?"*

As you see, the time and sign questions are the same as in Luke 21:7. Again, the reference is to "these things"—no *coming* is mentioned in Mark or Luke. His answers to the questions are in the same order as Luke 21:8-19. What the sign is *not* (Mark 13:6-13).

A. What the sign *is* (13:14-23)
  1. The "abomination that causes desolation" (the identity of this event is made very clear in Luke 21:20 with the participle "being surrounded").
  2. The Lord "cut short those days" (13:20). In a siege against the city lasting nearly a year, Cestius Gallius, the Roman general, withdrew to Caesarea and brought back a larger army. Thus, the alert Christians had the opportunity to flee (and Josephus, the Jewish historian and eyewitness to the event, says that many did, leaving the Jews in the city who were determined to fight to the death, which they did).[2]
B. The *time* question (13:24-32)
  1. Apocalyptic language is also used by Mark (13:24-27).
  2. The fig-tree parable (13:28-29). No *specific* time is given, but the *general* time is within *one generation* of approximately 40 years (13:30). However, no one knows *exact* time ("that day or hour"—13:32).
  3. Therefore, they needed to watch for the sign (13:33-37).

Matthew 24

Matthew's account of the questions about the destruction of the temple seems to be quite different than the other two accounts. A closer examination will reveal the differences to be in the language used, not in the substance of the message. Let's read Matthew 24:1-3:

> *Jesus left the temple and was walking away when his disciples came up to him to call his attention to its buildings. "Do you see all these things?" he asked. "I tell you the truth, not one stone here will be left on another; every one will be thrown down."*
> *³As Jesus was sitting on the Mount of Olives, the disciples came to him privately. "Tell us," they said, "when will this happen, and what will be the sign of your coming and of the end of the age?"*

If you read Matthew without reading the other accounts, you would immediately assume that three distinct questions are being asked.

1. When will the temple be destroyed?
2. What will be the sign of your second coming?
3. What will be the sign of the end of the world?

However, the questions are still two in number and they coincide perfectly with the two questions in Mark and Luke. They are merely stated in Jewish idiom.

A. The *time* question (*when*)
B. The *sign* question—stated in Jewish terminology, but it expresses the same question as in the parallels. As we will see, the question receives a two part answer.
   1. "Sign of your coming"—the word for "coming" is *parousia* in the Greek, meaning "presence" (24:3). Readers with a Jewish background would have taken these words to denote a coming in *judgment* (see the apocalyptic-style passages noted in connection with Luke 21, especially Isaiah 19:1). See Luke 19:44 for "the time of God's coming to you," a clear reference in context to the destruction of Jerusalem in 70 AD.

2. The "end of the age" (24:3). The word for "age" is
   from the Greek *aion* rather than from *kosmos*, the
   word for "world." Compare the reference to the
   "end of the age" here with the same phrase in
   Matthew 28:20.

The disciples could hardly have been asking about a second
coming according to our concept, since they did not think
Jesus was going anywhere! See Luke 9:45, 18:34—their
understanding of even his clearly told death was absolutely
nil. The word "end" here (24:3) is the same root word in Greek
translated "fulfilled" in Mark 13:4. The destruction of
Jerusalem was certainly a matter of the fulfillment of prophecy,
whether the apostles understood it well or not. The similar
use of "end" in Matthew 24:6, 14 refers to the same event,
which in its context points to the destruction of the city.

If the disciples were not asking about the second coming
and the end of the *kosmos*, what *were* they asking? Two
possible interpretations are:

A. The disciples assumed that such a great event would be
   the end of the Jewish world (or perhaps the whole
   world). If the *Jews* (23:34-36) and the *temple* (24:1-2)
   were to be destroyed, their world would end.
B. Since "coming" is from *parousia* ("presence"), often
   used in Greek to denote the arrival of a king, they may
   have pictured Jesus coming in battle against the
   Romans. Such an "arrival" would terminate the old age
   and usher in a new one. This view coincides with
   popular Messianic expectations of the disciples fairly
   well. Consider these words from John 6:14-15: "After
   the people saw the miraculous sign that Jesus did, they
   began to say, 'Surely this is the Prophet who is to come
   into the world.' Jesus, knowing that they intended to
   come and make him king by force, withdrew again to a
   mountain by himself." Either way, the question refers
   to "these things" as in Luke 21 and Mark 13. As Jesus
   said in Matthew 24:34 (emphasis added), "this
   generation will certainly not pass away until all *these
   things* have happened."

As Jesus' answers are recorded, they follow the same basic
approach as in Mark and Luke.

A. What the sign is *not* (Matthew 24:4-14)
   1. False christs (24:4-5, also 24:23-26).
   2. Wars (24:6).
   3. Natural calamities (24:7).
   4. Persecution to the point of death (24:9).
   5. Apostasy stemming from the love of most people growing cold (24:10-12).
   6. The gospel being preached in the whole world (24:14). (See Colossians 1:6, 23 for a first-century fulfillment of this prediction.)
B. What the sign *is* (24:15-28)
   1. The "abomination that causes desolation" (24:15). Remember that Luke 21:20 defined this event as the surrounding of Jerusalem by Roman armies, indicating that the desolation of the city and the temple was imminent.
   2. Christ's coming—which will be definite, in contrast to the coming of false christs (24:26-27).
   3. The location of this coming will be where the vultures gather (24:28) to devour a decaying carcass (most likely to be understood as Judaism). Compare this statement with Hebrews 8:13 and 12:25-29. Judaism with its sacrificial system was nearing its final end when all of these statements were made and written. Once the temple was destroyed, the sacrificial system was ended for all time.
C. The *time* question (24:29-36)
   1. Again, the use of apocalyptic language describes the end of the system (24:29-31).
   2. The *coming* will be "immediately" after the distress of those days. ("Immediately" is from the Greek *eutheos*, meaning "at once" or "soon," and it obviously refers to something which will occur shortly. Trying to fit in 2,000 years would strain the meaning of the word considerably!)
   3. "Sign" in 24:30 is from the Greek *semeion*, which refers to a "token" of something rather than the thing itself. In other words, a

signification of Christ's coming will be seen in the events he predicted and not the Son of Man in person.

4 "Mourn" in 24:30 is in the future passive tense and could be translated "mourn for themselves."

5. The angel gathering the elect (24:31) could refer figuratively to the preaching of the gospel to the world after the destruction, or it could refer to a gathering of the elect out of the city before its destruction (more probable). See the following verses for the concept of being gathered by God: Deuteronomy 30:4, Psalm 106:47, Isaiah 27:13, 45:22.

6. NOTE: The "coming on the clouds" and the "trumpet call" are associated with the second coming in certain other passages. However, this does not prove that they are meant to be applied in the same way here. For one thing, Revelation 1:7 uses these figures to indicate something other than the second coming, and for another thing, the context of Matthew 24 will not allow it.

7. The fig tree parable (24:32-33).

8. No specific time is given—the general time is:
   a. Within one generation (24:34).
   b. The certainty of Jesus' prophecy coming to pass is seen in 24:35. (Compare the wording with Luke 16:17.)
   c. Since no one knows the exact time (the day or hour), he was instructing them to pray that it not be in winter or on a Sabbath (24:20). Travel would be difficult in winter conditions, and leaving the city on a Sabbath was difficult because the city gates were closed in observance of the Sabbath.

9. Since the precise time could not be known, they needed to watch carefully for the sign (24:37-51).

10. The wicked are contrasted with Noah, the righteous (24:37-39). When the flood came,

Noah was not caught unprepared; only the wicked were. Therefore, the comparison to the destruction of Jerusalem makes perfect sense. Stay spiritually in tune and watch for the signs of impending destruction.

11. One is taken, and one is left (24:40-41). In the analogy, the wicked were taken, not the righteous. If this passage were applied to the second coming, we might have some basis for the rapture concept. However, Jesus is continuing his discussion of the destruction of the city and the need to remain alert. Then escape will be possible.
12. The admonition to watch is concluded in 24:45-51.
13. Three views of kingdoms are given in Matthew 24 and 25:
    a. The kingdom *destroyed* (Jewish system)—Matthew 24.
    b. The kingdom *remaining* (the church of Jesus Christ)—Matthew 25:1-30.
    c. The kingdom *eternal* (saints exalted at God's throne)—Matthew 25:31-46.

Luke 17:22-37

When I first began studying Matthew 24 and its parallels many years ago, Luke 17 posed a major problem to my interpretation of Matthew 24 at that time. The non-premillennial teachers I had heard normally divided this chapter into two major sections—the destruction of Jerusalem (17:1-34) and the second coming of Christ and the end of the world (17:35-51). Verse 36 was seen as a transition from the time of Jerusalem's destruction to the time of Christ's second coming. The focus was on the word "that." "No one knows about *that* day or hour, not even the angels in heaven, nor the Son, but only the Father" (emphasis added). I think the emphasis should be placed on "that *day and hour*," the *specific* time of the destruction of the city. (Incidentally, whatever the "coming" in view, we would assume the limitations of Jesus' knowledge here were due to his human limitations on earth. Once he ascended back to heaven, he would once again have omniscience.)

While the interpretation just described avoids the errors of premillennialism, it is impossible to harmonize with Luke 17. Although the surrounding context of Luke 17 is not a parallel to Matthew 24, Mark 13 and Luke 21, it does contain many of the same signs. Let's look at the difficulties of harmonizing these passages of Scripture. As we have stated, Matthew 24 is often divided into two major sections by Biblical scholars:

A. The Destruction of Jerusalem (17:1-34)—which we will call *Section A*.
B. The End of the World (17:35-51)—which we will now call *Section B*.

Notice what happens when Luke 17 is paralleled with Matthew 24, using the wording classed in *Sections A* or *B*: (Keep your Bible open and read these passages carefully!)

1. Luke 17:24	Matthew 24:27	(*A*)
2. Luke 17:26-30	Matthew 24:37-39	(*B*)
3. Luke 17:31-33	Matthew 24:17-18	(*A*)
4. Luke 17:34-36	Matthew 24:40-41	(*B*)
5. Luke 17:37	Matthew 24:28	(*A*)

Obviously, the signs in Luke 17 are mixed up considerably when compared to Matthew 24 and the parallel accounts in Mark 13 and Luke 21. Only three possibilities can be offered for this phenomenon in trying to make sense of Luke 17:

A. Luke 17 is a *jumble* which cannot be understood (which reflects negatively on the Holy Spirit who inspired it).
B. The entire passage refers to the second coming (a position with *multiple* problems). The same wording is found in Matthew 24 (and parallels) which definitely refers to the destruction of the city of Jerusalem in those contexts. And then why (and how) would someone go into their house for material goods (Luke 17:31) when Christ comes? The suddenness of the second coming and subsequent events would make such actions seem ludicrous. Lot is used as an example in Luke 17:28-29, which exactly coincides with the case of Jerusalem

where the righteous fled and the wicked remained to be destroyed in the city. In the day that the Son of Man is revealed (17:30), the watchful were to escape rather then go back to their homes (17:31). Of course, no such choices will exist when the second coming does occur!

C. All of Luke 17 refers to the destruction of Jerusalem. In light of all the evidence, this view is *by far* the most logical and consistent view. (It should be obvious that adopting this interpretation in Luke 17 necessitates viewing Matthew 24 and parallels in the same way.)

Endnotes

▼

Chapter 1

1. Albert Barnes, *Barnes Notes on the New Testament*, one volume, (Grand Rapids, Mich.: Kregel Publications, American edition, fifth printing, 1970) 15-36.
2. Hal Lindsey, *The Late Great Planet Earth* (Grand Rapids, Mich.: Zondervan Publishing House, 1970).
3. For a longer discussion of the fullness of time, see *The Eternal Kingdom*, F.W. Mattox (Delight, Arkansas: Gospel Light Publishing Company, 1961) 19-30.
4. For a fuller treatment of the historical development of emperor worship, see Homer Hailey, *Revelation: An Introduction and Commentary* (Grand Rapids, Mich.: Baker Book House, 1979) 59-90.

Chapter 2

1. For a fuller discussion of Matthew 24 and parallels, see Appendix 1, "The Destruction of Jerusalem," pp. 177-184.

Chapter 3

1. William Barclay, *Letters to the Seven Churches* (Nashville: Abingdon Press, 1957) 14-15.
2. Barclay, 41-42.

Chapter 4

1. Barclay, 101.

Chapter 5

1. A study of all titles or descriptions given Jesus in Revelation is a *revealing* study.

Chapter 8

1. New American Standard Version of the Bible.

Chapter 9

1. The material was originally included in my booklet and tape series on 1 and 2 Peter, *Refined by Fire*, page 22. I strongly recommend that you take the time to look up each of the following passages, make good notes about what you learn, and then spend some good time in prayer about how you view and react to rejection. Chapter 10.

Chapter 10

1. For passages showing this marital relationship, see comments in Chapter Three about the church at Thyatira.
2. Frank E. Peretti has written several describing this battle in the spiritual world. *This Present Darkness* (Westchester, Ill.: Crossway Books, 1986) is perhaps his best.

Chapter 11

1. See the brief exposition of the book of Hosea, *The Radical Edge* (Woburn, Mass.: Discipleship Publications International, 1994) 13-15.

Chapter 12

1. For a fuller discussion of the problem of good and evil, see my work, *The Victory of Surrender* (Woburn, Massachusetts: Discipleship Publications International, 1995), 167-180.
2. Christian Book Distributors, *Winter Clearance Sale*, p. 24.
3. *Winter Clearance Sale*, p. 25.
4. See Appendix 2 for an in-depth study of Matthew 24 and parallels, pp. 185-196.
5. Mike Taliaferro, *The Lion Never Sleeps* (Woburn, Mass.: Discipleship Publications International, 1996).

Chapter 14

1. *The Lion Never Sleeps* (see note 5 in Chapter 12) is a brief but powerful treatment of this concept.

Appendix 1

1. See the related discussion of "eternal" and "forever" in *Prepared to Answer*, pages 178-179.
2. Flavius Josephus, *The Jewish War*.

Who Are We?

Discipleship Publications International (DPI) began publishing in 1993. We are a nonprofit Christian publisher affiliated with the International Churches of Christ, committed to publishing and distributing materials that honor God, lift up Jesus Christ and show how his message practically applies to all areas of life. We have a deep conviction that no one changes life like Jesus and that the implementation of his teaching will revolutionize any life, any marriage, any family and any singles household.

Since our beginning, we have published more than 100 titles; plus, we have produced a number of important, spiritual audio products. More than one million volumes have been printed, and our works have been translated into more than a dozen languages—international is not just a part of our name! Our books are shipped regularly to every inhabited continent.

To see a more detailed description of our works, find us on the World Wide Web at www.dpibooks.org. You can order books by calling 1-888-DPI-BOOK twenty-four hours a day.

We appreciate the hundreds of comments we have received from readers. We would love to hear from you. Here are other ways to get in touch:

Mail: DPI, 2 Sterling Road, Billerica, MA 01862-2595
E-Mail: dpibooks@icoc.org

Find Us on the
World Wide Web

www.dpibooks.org
1-888-DPI-BOOK